I0478585

The Millionaire's Game
The Richest Man
In Jerusalem

GABRIEL EGOH

 iUniverse

The Millionaire's Game & The Richest Man In Jerusalem

Copyright © 2015 Gabriel Egoh.

All rights reserved. No part of this book may be used or reproduced by any means, graphic, electronic, or mechanical, including photocopying, recording, taping or by any information storage retrieval system without the written permission of the author except in the case of brief quotations embodied in critical articles and reviews.

iUniverse books may be ordered through booksellers or by contacting:

iUniverse
1663 Liberty Drive
Bloomington, IN 47403
www.iuniverse.com
1-800-Authors (1-800-288-4677)

Because of the dynamic nature of the Internet, any web addresses or links contained in this book may have changed since publication and may no longer be valid. The views expressed in this work are solely those of the author and do not necessarily reflect the views of the publisher, and the publisher hereby disclaims any responsibility for them.

Any people depicted in stock imagery provided by Thinkstock are models, and such images are being used for illustrative purposes only. Certain stock imagery © Thinkstock.

ISBN: 978-1-4917-7729-9 (sc)
ISBN: 978-1-4917-7730-5 (e)

Library of Congress Control Number: 2015914955

Print information available on the last page.

iUniverse rev. date: 09/09/2015

Contents

The Millionaire's Game:
Part One

Think Like a Millionaire

If you were given the sum of $200,000 or you earned that through some business transaction, how would you spend it? Can you multiply it two or three times or even to $10 million in five or ten years, assuming this opportunity would never come again? If you would like to think and spend like a millionaire, play this game by choosing how you spend your $200,000. For every option, refer to the corresponding number in appendix A to know its cost implication and market value in five years.

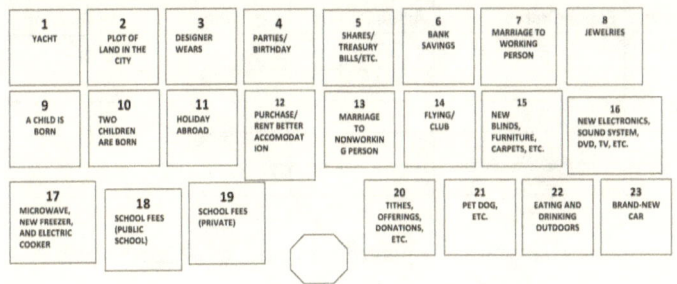

Example: This is how Mr. Eliezer would spend the $200,000.

	Year One	Amount		Year Five	Amount
No.	Expenditure	$	No.	Expenditure	$
25	New car	60,000	25	New car	-
4	Designer wears	45,000	4	Designer wears	-
12	Purchase/rent a better accommodation	50,000	12	Purchase/rent a better accommodation	-
6	Bank savings	10,000	6	Bank savings	100,000
17	Microwave New freezer	10,000	17	Microwave New freezer	-
16	New electronics Etc.	25,000	16	New electronics Etc.	-
	TOTAL	200,000		Total	100,000

Evaluation: Mr. Eliezer is a poor investor. He began year one with assets of $200,000, but at year five, he had only $100,000 worth of assets. Now try your hand at this game, and prove if you could multiply the original $200,000 to, say, $300,000, $400,000, or even an excellent fortune of over $2 million. If you can achieve this feat, you are on your way to millions. Then go on to play part two.

	Year One			Year Five	
No.	Expenditure	Amount	No.	Expenditure	Amount
		$			$

Now that you have played part one, go ahead to play two (PTO). By playing part two of this game, you will master the art of investing and building up your assets to become a multimillionaire. The game will test how you will invest between year six and ten. The test of a millionaire is over a period of time. In year six, you begin by investing your closing assets in year five, and for this purpose, it is assumed that your assets at year five could be easily liquidated to be invested in year six.

If we take the example of Eliezer in part one, he will begin year six with the assets of $100,000, the value of his assets at year five. For every option, refer to the corresponding number in appendix A to know its cost implication and market value in five years.

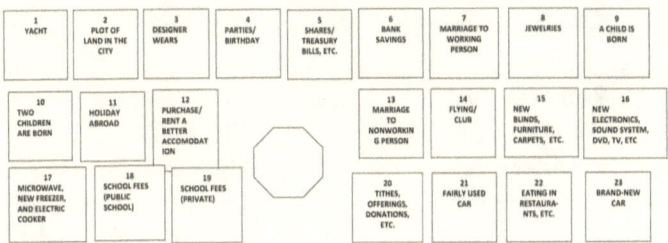

	Year Six			Year Ten	
No.	Expenditure	Amount	No.	Expenditure	Amount
		$			$
	Total			Total	

If you have mastered the art of investing and developed the millionaire's mentality at the end of year ten, you could have amassed well over $50 million in assets. Play this game several times over, and you will get to know the secrets of making millions.

Appendix A

(1) **Yacht**
It will cost $80,000, but it will be of no resale value in year five.

(2) **Plot of Lands in the City**
This land located in a fast-developing area of the city appreciates at 1,000 percent in five years. It costs $2,000 per plot, and it could be resold immediately and turned into cash for further expenditure or investment at the end of the five years. You could buy as much as possible.

(3) **Designer Wears**
It costs $45,000 over a five-year period, but it's of no value then. It costs $25,000 over five years.

(4) **Parties/Birthday**
It costs $100,000 over a five-year period, but it's of no value after that.

(5) **Shares/Treasury Bills, Etc.**
This could appreciate at 1500 percent over the five years and could be quickly turned into cash for further investments.

(6) **Bank Savings**
The yield is 200 percent over a period of five years.

(7) **Marriage to Working Person**
Income will increase $100,000 over the five-year period.

(8) **Jewelries**
It would cost $40,000, but it can only be sold for $90,000 in year five. This will cost $15,000.

(9) **Two Children Are Born**
This will cost $20,000.

(10) **Holiday Abroad**
This will cost $15,000.

(11) Purchase/Rent a Better Accommodation
This will cost an additional fifty thousand dollars. It will not be sold or valued at year five.

(12) Marriage to Nonworking Person
This will cost sixty-five thousand dollars.

(13) Flying/Club
This will cost twenty-five thousand dollars.

(14) New Blinds, Furniture, Carpet, Etc.

(15) New Electronics, Sound System, DVD, TV, Etc.
This will cost twenty-five thousand dollars, but it will be of no value in five years.

(16) Microwave, New Freezer, and Electric Cooker
This will cost $10,000, but it will be of no value in five years.

(17) School Fees (Public School)
This will cost $5,000.

(18) School Fees (Private)
This will cost $30,000.

(19) Donations
This will cost $20,000.

(20) Pet Dogs, Etc.
This will cost $30,000.

(21) Eating in Restaurants, Etc.
This will cost $30,000.

(22) New Car
This will cost $60,000, but it will be of no cash value in year five.

The Philosophy of the Millionaire's Game

Many pray they would come across a fortune in their lives so they might invest such to make more money. However, have you ever paused to consider the sum total of your income over a period of, say, five or ten years? Yes, although your income may come in trickles, week by week or month by month, it could amount to a fortune over a period of five or ten years.

Make a calculation of all your income from the past five or ten years. What can you show for all the revenue you earned over these years? While your income may have come in trickles over the years, you cannot be excused for not spending it judiciously or not engaging in investments that would better your lot in the future.

Some have been very fortunate to receive a huge sum from inheritance and others from the games table or lottery. For the generality of the people, fortune never comes at once. Rather by wisdom, they could save a certain percentage of their income, say, 10, 15, 20 percent, or more (depending on how they are able to control their expenditures) every month or so. In time, such savings become the fortune you could invest, as in the millionaire's game.

It means we have always had the opportunity to save and invest our income, whether our salary is little or large or whether they come in trickles or a lump sum. This is the philosophy of the millionaire's game. You don't have to wait until you have the millions before curbing or pruning your desire to reduce your expenditures and invest. You can begin in a very small way and watch your investment grow over the years. The urgent advice is for you to begin saving a portion of your income every month or so and then learn to invest either in shares, land, bank, savings, or other sources.

You could buy shares in trickles and save in tiny amounts. Of course you could also pay your mortgage in small payments. This is how to begin the journey into the millionaires. Don't wait for the sudden fortune, but begin now. Remember: a journey of a thousand miles begins with a step.

Chapter One

The Bitter Way to Learn and the Best Way to Riches

That night, my father, Arza, called to me and said to my face, "Moza, my son, I have watched with dismay all these years how you squandered my gold as if it had no source."

The seriousness on my father's face betrayed all his kindness to me since my youth. I carefully listened to what else would proceed from his heart.

Arza continued, "Now that I am no longer getting younger, I doubt if you would ever know how to build up stocks of gold. My son, you don't just spend gold, but you must know how to attract much gold to yourself. If you do this, your gold will never be exhausted."

Never in my life had my father spoken thus to me. He often gave me all I needed to enjoy my life as a young man. He never hesitated giving me gold to meet all my needs, even including those of my numerous friends.

But that fateful night, I began to hear different tones from my father. As my father kept silent for a while, my mind began to ponder such words as, *You squandered my gold. Build up stocks of gold.*

My heart was pounding as my father's lips moved to produce more words that pierced my heart like poisonous arrows. "I have thought things over and over again, and I have concluded that you don't know how to multiply gold. And if I pass on to the next world, you will exhaust all my gold in no time."

At this I opened my mouth and protested, "You have always taught others how to make and stock up gold, but never did you teach me."

My father then fiercely cut in, "My son, this is what I mean. The day has come for you to prove that you can make and even build up more gold on my wealth after I have passed on to the abodes of the gods. You are too naïve to be the heir to my wealth. Many a son has squandered great wealth left them by their parents. I tell you something. I will turn in my grave if you become a poor man, being the son of the richest man in Damascus. My decision is this. I want you to prove that you can earn gold and not only spend it."

My heart beat ever faster, and my tongue seemed glued to the roof of my mouth.

Arza said, "I will give you a scroll inscribed with the wisdom on how to control your desires and build up stocks of gold."

He paused a while, but I began to wonder in my heart, *What will come out of his mouth next?*

But before I could regain my composure, he added, "I will also give you a bag of gold and monitor you for a period of ten years to see if you can multiply it. Then I will trust you to be my heir."

When my father finished talking, he looked directly at my face as if he wanted to force a response from me. Beads of sweat rolled gently down my face, and I could sense the wetness at the back of my body as well. All of a sudden, I knew the game was up, and at least I must become a man capable of controlling my own destiny. After all, my friends had always teased me with the idea that I one day must begin to earn gold to cover my insatiable appetite for expenditures.

In reply, I said to my father, "You are Arza, the richest man in Damascus, the one whose store of gold is thought to be inexhaustible by even King Nebuchadnezzar. How then will you tell your son to earn gold whereas you have all the gold that would last all your life and forever?"

He looked down as if my words had struck a blow to his heart like an axe.

So I went further, "Don't you think, Father, it would be a shame if you sent me away to learn how to make gold?"

At this my father shouted, "Fool! Who told you that anyone has gold that cannot be exhausted? My gold looks inexhaustible because much more flows to me from my investments than I spend. If I were to turn my eye the other way while you spend the way you do, my gold would begin to deplete in no time. I fear greatly lest you make my wealth dwindle even before I pass on to eternity."

At these words fear gripped me, and I realized the only wise thing I could do now was to really prove to my father that I could earn gold and store it up, like he did to make him the richest man in Damascus. I thought to myself, *Now that my father will let me earn my own gold, I will not do it in Damascus. Rather, I will travel far and begin a new life.*

The day came when I wanted to depart for Nineveh. My father first handed me the scroll written with the wisdom on how to control one's desires, earn gold, and stock it for life. Then he looked me directly on the face, eyeball to eyeball for a long time, as if expecting a response from me.

Finally he handed me a bag of gold. He said with a husky voice, "Son, this scroll is more important than the bag of gold. Read it, memorize the inscriptions, and put them into practice. And then you will multiply much gold. Gold itself could be exhausted, but wisdom will bring it back." He concluded, "In ten years, I expect you to come to me with much more gold than I give to you this day if only you will read and understand the wisdom in these scrolls."

I mounted my camel as my father spoke on, and I directed my two slaves, Hezron and Bidkar, with their camels to move on. And as we rode past the boundary of Damascus, I asked one of my slaves how many years he thought it would take to exhaust the bag of gold if we earned none. He suggested the gold would last five years if carefully spent but would be exhausted quickly if I continued my kind of lifestyle in Damascus. I shook my head and began to wonder in my heart what I would do to multiply this bag of gold.

By now, we were descending into a valley where I saw some settlements. I suggested to my slaves to spend the night there. As we lay down that night, my heart became weighed down as the hot desert air blew over us. My mind raced back to my father's mansion in Damascus, where the maidens would fan me with fans made of long, rich ostrich or picked cock feathers. Now all that was gone in my quest to be a man. Just as the first rays of the sun broke forth from the direction of the east, I awoke my slaves to resume the long journey to Nineveh.

On a very hot afternoon on the sixth day of our journey, we ascended a hill. Then moving along a narrow pass, we could see the fortified walls of Nineveh well ahead of us.

My slave gestured toward the city and exclaimed, "That is the city of Nineveh."

At the far end, we could see a large river circling half the city wall. Here laid the strength and safety of the great city of Nineveh where commerce thrived.

It took us another full day before we got to the gates of Nineveh. Once in the city, we found an inn where we lodged for three months against the advice of my slaves that I should buy a house straightaway.

All these three months, I enjoyed my life, mixing freely with the rich and men of influence in the various inns that dotted such a great city. At last I noticed how quickly gold could flee from an extravagant owner. Worst of all, I learned that not only did gold flee from an extravagant owner; it fled even faster from one who had no means to replace it.

Six full months passed, and I discovered that half of my gold was gone. At this it occurred to me that it was time I earned some gold to multiply my stock back to me. As I enjoyed myself in the city, I saw people win large sums of money at the gaming tables in the inns. I thought that if I staked half of the balance of my gold, I could earn all the gold I lost in six months. In just one night, I lost all the gold I staked.

That night, I wept all through. Even my two slaves, Hezron and Bidkar, could not console me. When I looked at my bag of gold in the morning, only a quarter of what my father gave me was left. For the next month, I refused to attend any of the inns of Nineveh because I realized they were the source of the depletion of my gold.

I could hear the voice of my father from a distance saying, "Moza, my son, you only know how to squander gold, but you don't know how to earn it, and in no time, you would exhaust all my store of gold."

At once, as if by divine intervention, my mind was turned to look at the scrolls. I reluctantly glossed over them. Everything inside them pierced my heart, just as the words of my father Arza, the richest man in Damascus, would. The writings were so critical of my way of life that I felt guilty of having resisted every law of the acquisition and multiplication of God.

I thought to myself, *It's already too late to practice what is written in these scrolls.* But a second thought told me that the only way out was to practice the laws of gold and build up a stock. For days, I struggled within me to practice the laws of gold.

I began to tell myself that wishes were not enough, but immediate action was the answer. Of all the laws, the one that looked more like a big joke and seemed most impracticable was the one which read thus, "Anyone who must be rich must kill his desires. Desires swallow up gold like the grave that is never satisfied with dead bodies. List your desires, and you will find they are nurtured and sustained out of habit and emotions. Once you can kill your desire, you'll reduce the level of your expenditures to the extent your gold will be conserved."

As I read on, I began to wonder what I must do away with first. My mind raced to the beautiful maidens of Nineveh who had become parasites on my bag of gold by now. What about the expensive and palatable dishes I enjoyed much in the late evenings? These definitely also constituted a drain on my bag of gold. I could also remember how often I replaced my old—but not worn-out—garments for new and more fashionable ones from the faraway lands. By now, I knew I could have conserved all my gold if I had killed my desires and drastically reduced my expenditures. Like what the law of gold rightly puts it, I had thought all my expenditures were necessities that could not be done away with.

I was only a fool. I had to change new garments every now and then just because I must please the maidens of Nineveh and look fashionable amongst my peers. Oh! Yes, I thought every expenditure was normal or a necessity born out of emotions. I found out I could use my stock of clothes for another ten years without buying any new ones. My clothes were never old before I bought new ones just out of emotion and to appear fashionable.

What about the pretty maidens? I thought that if I loved my life, it was the right time I sent all those parasites packing. They specialized in making demands without contributing any shekel to one's life. It was not time for them. It was the moment to earn and multiply gold.

For days, I refused to visit the inns and bars where the maidens of Nineveh flocked daily to scavenge gold from the foolish like me. Surprisingly enough, many began to knock at the door of my residence to continue their extortion of gold from me.

I initially treated them with kid gloves, so they persisted until I got mad with them. Then they withdrew one by one, and I was relieved. These maidens didn't know if you were dying or going down the drain. All they wanted was gold, so if you didn't hit them hard, they'd only leave when they saw your corpse being lowered into the grave.

I could remember the words of my father, "I want you to prove that you can earn gold and not spend it. I will also give you a bag of gold and prove you for a period of ten years to see if you can multiply gold."

But now, a full year had passed without anything to show for it, but for the prostitutes of Nineveh, it was good-bye to them. If I must conserve my gold, I must also immediately stop the visits to these expensive lunch and dinners. While the slaves could prepare my meals for me at just a fraction of what I currently spent in these expensive inns, I could save much from that. I finally thought I could also conserve more of my gold by changing my residence from this bogus mansion of several bedrooms to an accommodation just enough to house my two slaves and me.

For hours, I battled with the thoughts of how best to cut my expenditures and conserve the quarter bag of gold left in my possession. Different options came to me. I must shelve the plans to buy another wagon. I could just maintain the one I came with from Damascus. All of a sudden, my way of thinking changed, and a new world opened up to me. I began to say over a hundred times within me, *I can do it.*

The battle line was now drawn. I would scrutinize all my expenditures over and over again and cut off those especially motivated by emotion, self-pride, women, and pressure from peer groups. I would critically look at them item by item and expenditure by expenditure until I made enough acts to conserve my gold. *As from today*, I said to myself, *no expenditure was a sacred cow. I would never again spend out of emotion, fashion, or just with the intent to please women or men.*

Now that I had succeeded in putting away the ravenous maidens and prostitutes of Nineveh, I realized I must also put a spirited effort to deal with friends and acquaintances who, one way or the other, also contributed to the depletion of my gold.

Some were attached to me like a tick would to a cattle, sucking his blood. In the bazaars where I frequented to purchase the latest garments, jewelry, or ornaments from faraway lands, they would mill around, hoping to get a gift from me. And indeed they did, so I became very popular. However, I had decided to stop all these kind of cheap popularity that led nowhere but poverty and rather save my gold.

In the inns, many sang my praises because I was always in the habit of paying their bills, but none ever paid mine because I was a fool. Everywhere I went in Nineveh, I was well known because of my foolish generosity to squander my gold. I said to myself, *I will no longer play the fool who lavishly doles out gold without returns.* I also often met the rich and very affluent who frequented these inns and bars just to while away time.

The question was, how I would face all these people if I stopped socializing with them? Anywhere they found me, they would like to question why I no longer visited the inns and bars. I had to find a way to answer them and preserve my gold.

I knew I was in a fix, but I was determined that wisdom must prevail. Initially, I thought all I could do was to pack my bag, bolt out of Nineveh at night, and begin a new life elsewhere. I later decided to face the situation with every desperation and boldness and not run away; else, I would be on the run all my life. *In a way, if I could do this, I had succeeded halfway*, I thought to myself.

When I stopped visiting the bazaars to squander my gold on the latest fashionable garments and other ornaments from faraway countries, I also cut off the hoard that often accompanied me hoping to receive gifts from me. It was quiet a savings.

Come to think about it, the less I spent, the more gold I conserved, and I was happy I safeguarded my gold. On some occasions when my affluent friends required me to explain my absence from the inns and bars, I earnestly and boldly told them that I could no longer sustain that way of life, and it worked.

So now that I had but little gold left, I had to be bold and sincere because if I did not, I would eventually do so in great shame if I totally became a poor man having exhausted all my gold. Initially the words were heavy in my mouth, but I suppressed all shame to tell them the truth so that if they were in position to help or counsel me, they would do so.

To my surprise, none cared about my predicament. All they seemed to say was, "See to it yourself, and learn wisdom." In a way, I could not blame anyone for my predicament. If you are wise and rich, everyone enjoyed or benefited from you, but if you are a fool, you die in your foolishness far outside the view of the public.

Separating therefore from those friends should have been no problem after all it. Because I had gold, they got to know me. The relationship was never borne out of genuine love, or so I thought. However, I was careful to sustain a few friends who could be beneficial to my business life. I could easily identify such acquaintances. They were very reserved and often quietly slipped into the inns and bars and discussed with the likes, and in a moment, they were out.

The few times I found myself in their midst, I was most uncomfortable and embarrassed. While they discussed wisdom and business, I had nothing to contribute. Fools were never comfortable where there was wisdom, just as the poor would be most embarrassed when they found themselves in the midst of the rich. And before long I could no longer stand the company of the wise and rich. While they discussed that art of making gold, I talked about just spending. I guessed they would have known I would someday go down the drain.

Oh! How I wished I stocked these groups of people. They would have helped to propel my life to some great heights.

Maybe they would have shown me one or more sources of making gold. Then my bag would have not been depleted. It was always too late to cry when the head was off.

I was getting ready to read and digest the other law of gold, which read thus, "Never put your gold to unrealistic earnings. By such, many have lost their gold to become slaves."

Yes! If I had obeyed this law, I would have not resorted to gambling to multiply my gold. I thought I could make it overnight by winning a jackpot. After all, a few were lucky to win. This was how I lost a quarter of my gold. I now realized that only a few ever won a jackpot after they had lost so much. Of a thousand, only a few ever won.

This was definitely a suicide bid. I didn't think I would ever leave my life to chance again. The laws forbid putting gold to unrealistic returns. I was a fool. I should have studied the scrolls that my father gave me before embarking on any spending spree. After all, my father first handed me the five scrolls of wisdom before the bag of gold. It was wisdom before money, but I had put the cart before the horse.

As I picked up the third scroll to study the third law of gold, one of my slaves, Bidkar, came in to announce the arrival of two men who wished to see me. I reluctantly asked them to come, as I was deeply engrossed with my studies. I asked my slave to let in the men. They did this diligently.

I then quickly asked the men to narrate their mission to me. The taller one amongst them began by introducing themselves, "We two are newly freed slaves of the richest man in Nineveh. Here are the certificates of our freedom." All the while, he poked the inscribed scroll rudely toward me.

"What then can I do for you?" I asked with an urgent voice.

The taller fellow continued very persuasively, "In times past, we drove our master in caravans once a year to some distant land where he bought gold ore. He came back to melt them into proper gold."

As he spoke, my face began to brighten up. A surge of interest engulfed my mind and asked him to continue.

"Sir, if you could finance the trip, you will make much bags of gold as profits."

No doubt, this was the kind of opportunity I was looking for. We quickly fixed the date for the long and tedious journey. In all, it took us seven days of travelling in the wilderness in some of the most hostile terrain I had ever seen. The journey was a big risk, as the desert Arabs were often laying in wait to rob the unsuspecting and weary traveler.

From a distance, I could see the workman toiling. Some were digging the side of the hill, while others washed some stones in drums. My two escorts, the so-called freed slaves, introduced me to some merchants there, and I bought as much ore as I could.

When I arrived back to Nineveh with my slaves, I quickly made my way to the experts who would refine the gold. On their thorough examination of the ore, their verdict was, "These are worthless pieces of stone."

All at once, I knew I had come to the end of the road. I later learned that these two so-called freed slaves were just dupes who went from stranger to stranger in Nineveh by enticing them into the dubious deals to rob them of their gold. At last what I feared most, poverty, had come upon me. But I said to myself, *I will not give up*. I headed toward my place of abode.

The third scroll of wisdom I was reading before the two strangers came knocking lay on my table. The fate that befell me had befallen many who came to sudden wealth, riches, windfall, an inheritance, and so forth. They knew how to spend gold but not how to replenish what they had spent contrary to the law of gold which said, "Gold flees very quickly from those who only spend without earning more to replenish what they have spent. Gold quickly accrues and multiplies to those who spend far less than they earn. Therefore, learn to gradually build up your gold because you then will also learn to control your desires to spend it rather than hope for a sudden windfall that you may not be able to maintain or which may never come at all." A glance at it read thus, "Do not invest your gold without the help of an expert unless you have a thorough knowledge of the venture."

I turned away from the clay tablet. As I was looking at the blank wall, tears began to roll down my checks. I said to myself, *If only I had read this third law of gold, I would not have lost all my gold.*

I could hear the voice of my father from distant Damascus, "Moza, my son, wisdom is better than riches. First, learn wisdom, and gold will flow to you like streams of river."

By now, every kind of thoughts flooded my mind, and I began to bite my finger at my regrets for not studying all the laws of gold before embarking on spending the bag of gold that my father gave to me. However, I knew I could still do something, read the balance of two laws of gold if by chance I might learn to recover all I had lost.

The fourth law read thus, "Gold will multiply to anyone who sets aside a minimum of a tenth or more of his income monthly or periodically."

I finally read the fifth law, "Gold will flow like a stream of river to the man who carefully invests it in some secured and trusted venture. Gold flees from the owner who wants to get rich quick. In time, great opportunities to make more gold will come knocking at the doors of those who have accumulated gold."

At that, I swore I would learn and memorize the five laws of gold and apply them to all I would embark upon in the future. The next day, I sold my camels, two slaves, Hezron and Bidkar, and stock of raiment so I could raise money to become a merchant. On my way home, I heard an uproar, and all people were running helter-skelter.

I quickly asked a passersby the meaning of what was happening. He explained that the poorest of the people were rebelling against the king's new law to increase their tax. They therefore had resorted to rioting and looting the stores of the merchants. He advised me to find my way to some secured place because in a couple of moments, the king's soldiers would be out, and anyone caught would be sold as a slave or even killed. The stranger quickly disappeared, but as I tried to make my way through some shanties, the king's men arrested me and robbed me of all that was on me.

The next day, I was sold as a slave to a man from a distant city. I never imagined living the life of a slave and not to talk about becoming one. My cruel and ruthless captors never listened to any plea or appeal. As I was being carried away in chains, I said to myself, *I will never give up.*

To me, life was full of ironies. A while ago, I was the rich master of two slaves, but now I had not only become a poor man but a slave. Initially, I thought to commit suicide to escape all the problems facing me, but another said, *Then you are a coward. Only fools escape from problems, but the wise and bold march on to always have the victory waiting for them.*

When I came to myself, I reasoned that I was where I was because of my foolish decisions yesteryear. If only I had learned the wisdom in the five scrolls my father handed me, I would have been a master and not a slave. So who did I blame for my predicaments? None else but myself.

My father told of how he failed to accumulate gold after ten attempts over a period of twenty years. But here I was, trying to give up just after a single failure. What a coward I was. Life was full of cowards. There were those who fail and quit. They never succeeded in life. I said to myself, *If my father failed ten times and did not quit, I will try as many times as possible until I succeed in earning and stocking up gold just like my father did.*

I had read in the scrolls that even slaves who had wisdom had very bright chances of making it in life. If he worked hard, he would become skilled or master of whatever trade he was assigned to. Such hardworking slaves were often made supervisors or overseers over others who were either lazy or carefree.

Eventually, my father said, "They would either be made partners or offered the chance to buy their freedom."

I could now vividly remember one or more such ex-slaves but now rich men as I squandered my gold in the inns and bars of Nineveh. I found something unique with former slaves who were now rich men. They were never ashamed to tell others who wished to hear that they were slaves in the past. I said to myself that wisdom teaches that one must make the best use of every situation, even the worst ones.

In fact, fools never learned wisdom until they were forced to do so. This was the exact situation that faced me. I was now compelled to learn wisdom so I would not only become rich but, most important of all, become the heir of the richest man in Damascus, my father, Arza.

When I had a bag full of gold, I was classified as one of the wisest men in Nineveh because all rich men were thought to be so. However, I was only a fool in disguise as I applied no wisdom in the way I spent. At last, when my gold was exhausted, it dawned on all that I was not a wise man despite all I had. Poor men were never accorded the luxury of being called wise men.

I sent to my father, the richest man in Damascus, to buy back my freedom.

He said, "Moza, my son, life is a journey or school through which you must pass through and learn wisdom. The tougher the situations one faced, the more the chances of learning new things that will shape him for a better life in the future. Whatever one has learned will never be a source of failure any more. If I bought you your freedom, you would be the most miserable man on earth since you would have lost the chance of learning wisdom but at the same time also face the problem of managing my vast rich interests because you don't have the wisdom to manage gold.

"What joy will it be to you if I willed my wealth to a stranger who is wiser and more capable than you are? I would rather prefer to do this than see a foolish son squander all the gold I labored for all these years. Many a foolish sons have indeed done evil to their dead parent by extravagantly lavishing all that their parents labored for.

"I will not allow this to happen to me because you would suffer, and the society we live in would also bear the adverse consequences. Think about the thousands that would lose their income and means of livelihood should a foolish son destroy my estate.

"Wealth benefits not only the owner, but it does more to the society than you ever thought. I therefore owe both you and society a duty to preserve my gold. Many a slave has worked hard, and the richest men learned enough wisdom to not only buy their freedom but have also become some of the richest men in Damascus.

"Son, I refer you to the wisdom in the five scrolls. Read and memorize them. Then apply everything about them to your life, and in no time, you will become one of the wealthiest men that ever lived. Remember: when you come back successfully, my great wealth awaits you. So learn wisdom very quickly."

Just as my father had sent to me that slavery was a school, I became more determined to pass through it in flying colors so I would eventually become an expert at managing gold in the future. I never felt bad about my father's position. Rather, I saw a chance for me to become what he wished me to be, his heir, and to be useful to both myself and society at large.

Our hours of work were often very long, but I always put up additional efforts so I could master whatever trade I was assigned to. Other fellow slaves would grumble and query why I worked so hard. To me, they were just a lazy bunch who would rather destroy than build.

My hard work paid off. In no time, I mastered the art of working on metals and gold. While other slaves were lazing around, I steadily kept the pace of my labor. Then my master noticed my industry made me the supervisor of all his metal business. To me, this was the first success story, and I hoped to capitalize on it. I indeed craved for more recognition from my master.

I longed to be a free man, knowing fully well that in six years I must report my ability to earn gold and stock it to my father. However, I did not allow my thoughts of freedom to cloud my thinking and hinder the tempo of my efforts.

As usual, I worked even harder as a supervisor, especially when I remembered the words of my father, who often told me there was dignity in labor. My master had no regard for all the other slaves because of their attitude to work, but he trusted me and treated me kindly.

I could actually see that my hard work had earned me the post of a supervisor and a position of trust. By now, my master began to pay me some wages despite the fact that I was his slave. I did not forget the laws of gold all these years, so I was saving virtually all my earnings since I had free food and accommodation. The other slaves watched me with envy, but I cared less about them because they were not willing to work hard. Month after month, I watched my savings of shekels grow.

At the second year, I had enough savings in gold to buy my freedom. In time, I approached my master for freedom, which he did grant me without hesitation but suggested I become his partner in the metal business. I had expected this because he was aging and without children of character to be his heirs. He had other vast business interests that required more of his attention. I gladly accepted the offer to become a partner with my master, and in this I prospered greatly, and my stock of gold grew very quickly.

I was very diligent in handling my store of gold, and I avoided all the pitfalls of the past that made me squander the bag of gold my father gave me. I was no longer a fool because

I was daily reciting the laws of gold, which were inscribed in the scrolls that my father gave me.

I was also very eager to practice the laws of gold, and it worked for me. Sometimes when I looked at the past, I would regret and say to myself, *I wished I had begun practicing the laws of gold when I had the bag of gold*. However, this did not bother me much because I had learned my lesson, although in a hard way.

Because of my past and the future hope, I guessed I had become more determined. I would only invest my gold back in my business, and I put the balance in care of the moneylender to earn interest.

Many people came to give me different business proposals, but I rejected them because I knew little about them. Moreover, I was already earning reasonable returns on my current investments. From my past experience, I made up my mind never to get involved in any business in which I had no form of control or knowledge or anything get-rich-quick.

As the years passed by, I accumulated much gold and thought I could do better if I had my own business. I resigned the partnership and moved back to Nineveh, where there were particularly no experts in metal and gold works. I knew the market in Nineveh would be such that I would make gold faster than anywhere else could. Once settled in Nineveh, I invented a better mousetrap and locks, and I prospered very much. Everything my father had told me, I put it into practice, and it had become true in my life. One truth I found out was that a man in hurry could not be patient enough to make gold grow. Gold must nurtured like a tree over time until it begins to bear valuable fruits.

The king even took notice of me because of the quality and durability of my products. Many merchants came from faraway countries to buy my products. I enlarged my works and got more hands engaged to meet orders. I made sure that all excess gold with me was handed over to the moneylender to loan to the merchants. I therefore was earning from my metal works and interest from the moneylenders.

A time came when even the earnings from the moneylenders was in excess of what I got from my metal works. My money was working for me. It was easier to earn through your money working for you than your own efforts. I discovered this truth.

Eight years after I left Damascus, I had earned two bags of gold. I thought to myself, *I could add one more to it before I met my father on the tenth year.*

One day, just as usual, I was in the shop selling mousetraps, locks, and other articles to merchants from faraway cities. As I looked at the faces of the different merchants, your guess was as good as mine. You could tell who was standing before me to make an order. It was Hezron, one of my ex-slaves. He had heard about the quality of my products in Sidon and come to make an order.

I could instantly recognize him, but he never knew who I was. When I shouted his name, he immediately recognized me. We hugged each other for a long time. I asked about his well-being, and he told me he had regained his freedom and was now a wealthy merchant in Sidon.

Chapter Two

Everyone Is Born Equal But Riches Come by Choice

My father was born a slave and died a slave as well. By the virtue of my father's social status, by birth, I, Hezron, was automatically a slave. Just as my father did, I served Arza faithfully, and I was always attending to him when he gave lectures at his school of wisdom. I often listened with interest to his sermons, but I never thought they were meant to transform the mentality of a slave. So year after year, I listened to Arza, whose lectures turned paupers wealthy, but for a slave, to me, there was no hope. And on one occasion, I was so wrapped up in the lecture that I forgot appropriately to serve my master.

Arza looked at me, shaking his head. "Hezron, anyone could earn and stock up gold."

It was several years before I remembered what my master Arza said, not at the lecture hall this time, but as I watched his son Moza squander his bag of gold in Nineveh. I said to myself, *Very soon, Moza would finish his gold and become a slave like me.*

I therefore concluded that anyone could become a slave and any person could also become a master depending on how he faces the issues of life. I discovered that you are only a slave if you had the mentality of a slave, but if you were a slave and had the vision and mentality of a noble, you became one in the near future. So I changed my mentality that day, which changed my reasoning and approach to life.

Just as Moza was being weighed my purchase price by my new master, I began to recite in my mind the words of Arza's lecture on how to earn gold and make it work for you. This time around, I looked straight at Moza's face, but shaking my head, I queried in my mind, *Is this the son of the richest man in Damascus about to go the way of all fools?*

Moza had squandered all his gold. To meet his extravagant way of life, he had to sell his slaves and camels as a last resort. But from the look of things, I knew it would go further than that as he marched into poverty. But I knew the only way to halt his downward slide was for him to change his lifestyle by practicing the wisdom in the five scrolls that his father gave to him.

As I mounted the camel of my new master and we rode away out of Nineveh, word for word, I began to recite Arza's wisdom in my mind on how to make gold and stock it up. I could still recite the lecture off hand despite the fact that I heard it some ten years ago.

"Anyone on earth can become rich in gold, buildings, lands, and so forth, if only he understands that he must keep a portion of his income to himself before incurring any expenditure. We make two types of payment: payment to yourself and payment to others. Any payment you make to yourself makes you rich, while the payment you make to others makes you poor. What is the payment you make to yourself? It's savings or any other payment that makes you earn income. What's the payment you make to others: rent, food, clothes, fees, transport, and so forth. You make these payments to other people. It goes out of your pocket to make you poor, but what you keep for yourself as savings makes you happy and rich."

As Arza would persuade his students to do, "You could put away 10, 15, or 20 percent or even more of your income, depending on how much control you have over your desires. You will do much favor to yourself by putting away much to yourself. This is all you can show for your labor over the years.

"What you pay to others is lost to outsiders forever, and in most of the cases, you only enjoy such benefits for a short period of less than three years. Clothes would soon get old and become torn. Shoes soon wear out. The rent expires so soon only for you to pay more. The benefits you derive from paying others is short-lived and easily cleared from your memory. This is the sad story.

"But consider the portion of income you put aside to pay yourself, maybe 10, 15, or 20 percent or even more. You can see them physically with your eyes and feel them with your hands, and they give you joy and a sense of fulfillment. If you guard them with care, they last from generation to generation and grow infinitely into great wealth through wise investment."

He advised not to allow our desires to swallow up all our income so the portion you keep for yourself will be large enough to yield you great income. In any case, Arza advised that we pay ourselves before paying others. It was like the lion or tiger. He would eat his fill from the kill before inviting others.

"Satisfy yourself before others," he would drum into the ears of his students so it would not amount to greed or selfishness, nor lead to harassment from outsiders. He added quickly, "Who is more important to you: the outsider or your very good self?" He concluded, if you consider your good self to be more important, pay yourself before others.

In other cases, he put the question this way, "Paying yourself first and the outsider last, which will make you poor or rich?"

The answer was always obvious. You were better off when you paid yourself first. Suppose after paying yourself, there was not enough of your income to pay all the other expenses.

"What would you do?" he once asked a student. "Yes, those unpaid will run after you, demanding their due, but this gives you the opportunity to either kill your desire the more, or you will be pressured and motivated to look for other source of income."

As usual, all the students would burst out in applause.

In several of his lectures, the one that caused the most agitation in me was when he talked about the volume of income that people earned over the years.

As he said, "Could you imagine what your savings would amount to in two, five, or ten years when you put away 10, 15, or 20 percent or more of your income? By putting away 10 percent of your monthly income at the year-end, you would have saved a month's wages. 20 percent savings will give you two month's wages, while 50 percent savings will amount to six months of wages. All these savings will become your gold, but the one you paid to others is lost forever."

He pressed further, "The majority of people cannot believe how they spent their income at the end of every year. This is the sad story that they are not bold enough to investigate. However, if you kill your desires and do a good saving, happy are you at the end of the year, but the spendthrift is ever sad, uncertain, and confused.

"Gold coins in your saving box make you happy and self-confident, but they will not multiply. Only misers are satisfied with such, just worshipping gold. They are very conscious and fearful not to lose any gold but miss all opportunity to make it grow. They are fearful and live a life of uncertainty all their days. They become stagnant and miss all opportunities to invest and make their gold grow, thereby becoming mediocre. The very rich make their gold work for them. When you work by your accumulated gold or savings, it will work and earn income infinitely for you.

"This is the secret of the rich. They have their gold working for them, while the poor labor it out all their lives without anything to show for it. Get your gold invested with the help of experts who have proven knowledge about gold and not with hunches or incomplete information, and let it work for you. Then also allow their earnings to work for you and so on. Your income will know no bounds, and you will become very rich.

"This is another secret of the rich. They employ their gold and earnings to work for them. When their gold gives birth, they don't just consume it but also employ the children and grandchildren until a continuous flow of gold comes to them. Then they acquire whatever their hearts desire. The rich feast on the flow and not on the gold working for them. This is another secret of the rich. But the poor consume all their gold.

"Never get tempted to eat the children or grandchildren, but get them reinvested so your earning would be great in the future. I did exactly this when I was a poor wage earner. At the beginning when my gold began to have children, I was tempted to spend them on new raiment, women, perfumes, wine, and other beautiful things displayed by the merchants.

"But at last my mentor made me understand that the children and even the great-grandchildren of my gold must work to earn for me. He said there and then, 'Must I dare put my hand to the earnings to satisfy my desires.' The greatest reason why people lose their gold is because they are greedy to make it overnight. They do so by demanding unreasonably high and unrealistic or proven returns. Unreasonably high earnings are like gambling, which always result in losses. Whatever stock of gold you have is very precious. Hold it with care, and don't invest it in unreasonable or dubious ventures.

"We have now come to the most important aspect of why 95 percent of the people are poor and only 5 percent are rich the world over. The rich know how to control their desires, but the poor don't know how to do that. Most people wish, if there were increase in income, that they would easily and gladly set a tenth or more of it apart as savings. This has been found out to be untrue.

"Every increase in income will generate a new string of greedy desires waiting to consume them. Getting a second or third job does not necessarily mean that one will first pay himself. The law of poverty is, 'Every increase in income will generate a new sting of desire to consume them.' This is where the problem lies. The only way out is for us to systematically kill our desires."

Arza would advise, "Don't ask for pay increase. First learn to pay yourself. What is the use of an increase if you won't pay yourself first but pay all to others? Once you can master your desires, you have found the way to building up your stock of gold. Gold flows to those who set apart a tenth or more of his income to invest. Desires are not respects of persons. Either you kill them and build up a stock of gold, or they overwhelm you, consuming all your income and making you poor.

"You therefore don't feel emotional, restrained, or too conservative to trim your desires. The poor often strive to satisfy all their desires, but that is not so with the rich. The rich don't attempt to satisfy all theirs, and that does not necessarily mean that one will first pay himself. The law of poverty is, 'Every increase in income will generate a new sting of desire to consume them.' This is where the problem lies. The only way out is for us to systematically kill our desires."

Arza would advise, "Don't ask for pay increase; first learn to pay yourself. What is the use of an increase if you won't pay yourself first but pay all to others? Once you can master your desires, you have found the way to building up your stock of gold. Gold flows to those who set apart a tenth or more of his income to invest. Desires are not respects of persons. Either you kill them and build up a stock of gold, or they overwhelm you, consuming all your income and making you poor.

"You therefore don't feel emotional, restrained, or too conservative to trim your desires. The poor often strive to satisfy all their desires, but that is not so with the rich. The rich don't attempt to satisfy all their desires because, if they did, they would become poor. But the poor try to, so they cannot have saving.

"Desires are the number-one enemy of one who wishes to have much gold. Either you kill it or it kills you. The desire to buy something new, rent a more expensive apartment, replace malfunctioning furniture, buy more appliances, or shower more gold on family comfort will rob you of the gold you would set aside to invest to earn more gold.

"One evil I have seen is that poor people often want to spend like rich people so they can be seen as rich. They do this out of pride to hide their inferiority complex. Why must you spend like a rich man when you are a poor man? Simply, the poor actually want to become rich or thought of as being rich by the public. However, many do not want to make the sacrifices that make them rich. The poor wish to be rich, but they are not willing to turn their wishes into gold. What do I mean by poor? A poor man is without gold coins stacked away as investment.

"No matter the size of your current income, if you have no gold working for you, the one who earns less but has the gold mother and its children working for him is better off. So poverty is not defined in terms of what you earn now but as to what you invest to earn for you. If your desires eat up all the gold you earn each month, you are a poor man, no matter the size of your income, but if you have mastery over your desires, greatly curb your expenditure, and begin to build up stocks of gold, you are on the path to riches.

"We can do without much of our desires. They can be pruned or discarded, depending on how determined we are to be rich. All men are equal, but the ability of men to prune their desires makes the difference. Remember: rich people do not satisfy all their desires. They seem to spend much, but they are careful to limit their expenses to some determined amount such that they don't deplete the stock of gold working for them. But poor people want to satisfy all their desires;

hence, all their income is consumed and do not have any investments.

"A second thought will show that you don't have need for so many desires. You can invest your gold to earn more gold for you and then reinvest the earnings, even its grandchildren, to create a flow of earnings into your storeroom. The cheering news is that we cannot only curb our desires. We can, in fact, prune them. The day you begin to prune your desires, to reduce your expenditures, you will have gold coins accumulating in your pocket.

"Much gold awaits to be enjoyed by those who don't spend their gold now but invest it, their children and grandchild, to create earnings. Fools spend all their earnings of gold now on things, which do not last more than a year or two or three. They forfeit the gold that will multiply in the future to those who refrain from current expenditures but invest to build up their stock of gold. In order to reduce your expenditures, you must reorder your lifestyle by reducing all your expenses. By doing this you will have surplus gold to put to work for you.

"There is a limit to which your labor can earn for you, but your investment or surplus gold can earn you all the gold you ever desired. There is another definition of who is a poor man and who is a rich man. Poor men are those who earn their income by their own labor, but rich people earn their gold by making their gold the children of their gold and their grandchildren and so forth. Work for them.

"This is why there is a limit in the earnings of a poor man, but that is not true of the rich man because, the more gold he earns, he must therefore curb his desires and prune his expenditures so he can have more of his earnings invested to earn for him. In time, the mother, children, grandchildren, and so forth will form a team of gold laborers who work for you whether you are awake or asleep.

"More gold flows to those who already have gold, but gold flees from those who do not know how to keep a portion of their earnings to invest wisely. Opportunities often knock at the doors of those who have gold. Once in a while, there is a cheap bargain or someone in desperate need of cash or some other opportunity. Then the one with savings of gold cashes in to make huge profits.

"Opportunities are flying around daily, but those without wisdom and gold cannot profit by it. Such opportunities are never available to the ones without gold or the poor. As you build up your stock of gold over the years, opportunities are searching you out. Because gold belongs to God, he gives it to those who already have much of it. Those that have shall be given more because they know how to make it grow."

Arza gave this lecture to the pupils of his school of wisdom. As a slave attending to him, I dared not ask a question, yet I put them in my memory, waiting one day for an opportunity to express them. I never forgot them, and on this fateful day, I became the slave of a new master. I recited them as we rode on the back of the camel to Damascus.

Twenty years had gone by, yet the wisdom of Arza, the richest man in Damascus, never left me. With this knowledge in me, I even felt better than any free man because a free man is not free until he had learned to build up stocks of gold.

In Damascus, I worked very hard for my new master, but he was very cruel and heartless. He was unlike Arza or Moza, his son. We worked long hours, and he cared not whether you were ill or healthy. He often worked some slaves to death. Because I always remembered the wisdom of Arza, I often put up my best even at the worst of facilities and motivation.

Most important of all, I considered all my hard work and diligence the process of learning skills. So I learned the skills of leading caravans and the art of buying and selling distant goods from my master. While my master sold off lazy and sickly slaves, he kept me for my industry.

Hundreds of times, we travelled to Sidon, Jerusalem, and other distant cities to trade. But I longed to be a master of myself.

Day and night, I dreamed of freedom from slavery to practice the wisdom of Arza and become the owner of much gold.

At no time did I ever cease dreaming of freedom, yet I worked even harder for a wicked master who forgot no evil and rewarded no good. One day as we travelled in our caravan to Sidon, I suddenly pretended to be ill and slipped off the camel's back. There I lay on the ground, pretending to be unable to stand, talk, or regain consciousness. My master disembarked, and with the help of the other slaves, they tried to revive me but to no avail.

My master, suspecting I might have been pretending, hauled a jar of water at my head, but I pretended even the more that I was helpless. As they sensed he could do no more, each mounted his camel and left me to die in the wilderness.

For a while, I thought that was the end of my life, but I made sure they had gone several miles before attempting to sit up. By then the hyenas were closing up on me with the vultures hovering above to make a kill. I managed to sit up and hauled the first stone at them. Cowards! The hyenas fled, so the vultures disappeared likewise.

As I stood up, I shouted with a very loud voice, "I am free at last."

But my head and all my body ached badly. So I laid down once more to fully recover. I was motionless for a while, and this made the hyenas think I was probably very weak or dead, so they came back attacking one more time.

I summoned all my power. Lifting up a large chunk of rock, I hit one of the animals, destroying the snout and the jaw. It fell down dead. All the others fled once more, but this time never to return. For a while, I thought a dead hyena was worthless, but I remembered in our journeys that each person often carried a dagger and a source of fire, and all those things were present on me.

Just as pangs of hunger were encroaching on my stomach, I immediately skinned the animal, pieced it, and began to roast and dry some for the seven-day journey to Sidon. I looked around and found some more sticks. I lit another fire to scare off wild animals, and I slept as a free man for the first time in my life.

The next morning, the noise of the vultures attempting to steal the dry piece of meat woke me up. As I stood on my feet, for the first time, it dawned on me that as a free man. I must now cater for myself, and gone were the days when my master provided all my necessities. I said to myself, *I must now adapt to my new status.*

It was the irony of life. While the slave master fed and cared for the slave, a free man must meet all of his needs. No wonder some so feared freedom and chose to remain slaves. Was it not why the poor remain working with their labor rather than making use of their minds to allow gold to work for them?

Piercing the chunks of dried meat through with a long stick and then carrying it on my shoulder, I began the long and tedious matched toward Sidon. At sunset, I made two bonfires again, one to dry the pieces of hyena meat and the other, as usual, to scare off wild animals. Then I lay down, sleeping like a baby all night. The next day, I was on the move again. For another seven good days, I struggled along with worn-out saddles and feet until I finally got to the gate of Sidon.

As I sat down besides the city gate, I was determined to live a life of a free man, but this meant dumping every slave mentality that had overwhelmed me these past forty years of my life. One might be physically free, but with a slave mentality, you were not truly free to lead a meaningful life. Now, I must stand on my own and begin to earn some income. To a former slave used to eating the crumbs at the master table, this was a great responsibility.

While I was a slave, I only needed to work hard daily, but feeding, clothing, and so forth were not my worries but the business of master. Slaves, free men, and women were moving here and there for their businesses. At last I sat, thinking how to approach a newly discovered life. My thoughts raced to and fro like a fast-flowing stream.

The question was, where would I start from? One mind was suggesting to me that I could not face the affairs of life as a free man—that is, I should just offer myself to any willing slave master as a slave. For a while, I thought about this, but I said no. I was determined to remain free and become wealthy as I remembered the words of Arza, the richest man in Damascus, "Anyone could build up stocks of gold."

I regained my energy. A thought crossed my mind: what about offering the dried pieces of the hyena for sale at the marketplace? At first, I doubted if anyone would be interested, but I said to myself that a trial was worth it. If it worked well, I had gotten something to start with, but if otherwise, I could find an alternative.

Life was full of trials, and only those who don't will not win. If I didn't try at all, I could never win, but if I tried and lost, I could just keep trying until I won someday. If I did not try at all, I would have lost all chances of winning and remaining a failure. I moved straight to the marketplace and offered the last five big chunks of the dried hyena meat for sale.

The response of buyers was spontaneous, and in a moment, I had a few pieces of copper in my hand to begin the journey to wealth. I quickly made for two goatskins with which to fetch water from the river to sell to residents. There was dire need for water, like other big cities. After payment, I was glad some copper balances were still in my pocket. I said to myself, *I would start the business of selling water tomorrow to earn some copper and put Arza's wisdom into practice.* In just one month, my pocket was jingling with the copper coins. I put aside a third of all I earned daily. Some days were good enough for me to save half of the earnings.

Six months passed. I thought to myself that I would buy a slave who would, along with me, fetch water from the stream to sell. I promptly did this, and my earnings began to multiply. In no time, I acquired a second slave, and my gold increased greatly.

One night, I came home late after having a good time at one of the popular inns in the city of Sidon. My two slaves seemed fast asleep on a heap of hay they often used as a bed, but I dived right on my comfortable Damascusian rug and began to slumber immediately. Much wine made me sleep deeply, and I became totally oblivious of all happenings around me. In my sleep, I began to have a dream that a golden chariot drawn by two white horses crushed me.

This dream startled me. At once, I jumped on my two feet, but it was already daybreak, and the bustling city life had begun. As usually, my slaves would have already gone several rounds supplying water to our customers, so I was not disturbed about their absence. But what created sudden fear in my heart was the disappearance of my chest and bag of raiment.

Out of curiosity I moved into my slave's apartment. I discovered everything in there was packed clean and the room was empty. I needed no other proof. My two slaves had escaped into freedom with all my savings of gold for two years. I sat there and wept until no energy was left in me.

Now, I must start all over again because no copper was left on me. I should have not kept all that money with me. I should have invested the money with a lender or loaned it to the merchants and earned much income within the period of two years. *It would have been safe*, I said to myself. *This is the fate of all misers. They love gold for gold's sake.*

I watched my gold grow in admiration, not considering what it would yield if it worked for me by investing it. Now I thought I was wiser having lost so much. I moved around my entire water customers, hoping one might lend me some copper coins to purchase new goatskins, but none listened nor sympathized with me.

I regretted for not applying the wisdom of Arza in my finance. Arza would tell his students, "Guide your capital jealously so you don't lose it; else you'll start life all over again." He said, "Your capital is your life." Therefore, I just lost my life as my slaves made away with all my savings in gold.

What a pity. No one was ready to help me start all over again. I was a fool for hoarding all my gold for two good years like a miser without investing it in other profitable ventures to allow the mother, children, and grandchildren to work for me.

The sayings of Mr. Arza had caught up with me. "The poor work to earn gold, but the rich make their gold work for them." Herein I failed again to apply the wisdom of Arza. I now thought, *If I could just once more build up my business, I will strictly apply the wisdom that Arza gave me.*

Now none of my water customers would borrow me a copper to buy goatskins. *So what would I do?* I asked myself. *I could go to the sellers of goatskin to see if they would agree to a deal.*

I went to the sellers, and they agreed to sell to me but at triple the price. I immediately grabbed the opportunity because that was the only option I had. I was to pay by installments for twelve months. I also agreed to do this. The next day, I started my supply again, and I was glad that copper coins began to fill my pocket once more.

I promptly kept a tenth of my earnings to myself, and I committed a fifth toward paying my debts. I continued this for six months, by which time I completely paid the debts I incurred in buying the goatskins. The tenth I saved for six months, I took to the moneylender, who lent them to the merchants of Sidon.

In return the moneylender paid me quarterly for its use, but instead of me spending the interest, I gave it back to the moneylender, who reinvested it by lending it to the merchants. I did this for a period. In time, I employed several more slaves and free men as my business grew. My balance with the moneylender continued to grow until it was equivalent to half a bag of gold.

At this the moneylender called me to take over the business of a bankrupt merchant who could no longer pay back his loans. The agreement was that I would be with the merchant, selling and travelling in his caravan for six months until I mastered the trade. Then I would fully take over the business.

For that period of time, I did learn a lot from the merchant, and because I had much money I had invested with the moneylender, I needed not borrow to trade. Although business was good and I made much gold, I never once ceased giving a tenth or more of my earnings to the moneylender. By this, I avoided putting all my earnings into buying and selling, but a tenth or more of it, I gave to the moneylender to lend to needy merchants. Either way, my gold grew.

All these days, I mastered my desires because I knew that if I pursued them, my capital and earnings from trading would be depleted. While others bought new chariots, I maintained my old one. I bought new garments only when my old ones were getting worn out. Every now and then, more fanciful garments and ornaments were brought to me from faraway cities, but I refused to be interested because that would reduce the gold I paid myself.

I always said to myself that a day would come when I would afford all these things without any effect on my savings in gold. I never spent on emotions; nor did I pursue vain expenditures on account of fashion or women. This was how I built my business, and much gold flowed to me.

An official of the king once approached me to buy some of the king's forest and fell timber for house beams and furniture, but I declined this because I knew nothing about trees. In another occasion, some fishermen proposed my buying a fleet of fishing boats. I also declined this because I could not go to sea; neither did I have knowledge of fishing. To me, the selling of water was easy, so I went into it while I knew I could learn the arts of the merchants in six months.

I made it a policy by drawing from the wisdom of Arza to never be involved in what I technically knew nothing of. I had a grasp of all I did and could determine if I were profiting or not.

I shunned the tables of the gamblers or anything to do with excessive returns because, by the risks inherited in such business, one could easily lose his capital. It was better to earn little and steady returns and preserve your capital than to aim too high and lose your life savings. Because of the wisdom of Arza that I hid in my mind, I conducted my affairs diligently and with great care.

In time, many good opportunities came to me, and because I had built my stock of gold all over the years, I was able to cease such and multiply my stock of gold very much.

Sometime ago, all the animals in Sidon died of a strange disease, and there was a shortage of beef in the city. It was necessary to bring in animals from faraway places, but none of the merchants had enough gold to do so. But since I had diligently built my stock of gold all the years, I invested all the necessary gold to bring in all the animals required. Through this I doubled my stock of gold in just six months.

In another occasion, the city had so grown in population, and farmland became so scarce and expensive that I bought new lands from the king, demarcated them, cleared them of stones, and leased them to the farmers, who agreed to pay my the lease with a fifth of their produce for life. The farmers were happy because they put no cash down, but I became rich through them as I was a recipient of their produce for life.

Arza said, "Great opportunities knock at the door of one who has much stock of gold."

"So my brother Moza, my ex-master, this was how I conducted my affairs according to the wisdom of Arza, the richest man in Damascus, and I also became the richest men in Tyre and Sidon."

***

All the while Hezron narrated his path to much gold, Moza listened to how an ex-slave used the wisdom of his father, Arza, to become the owner of much gold. Moza, beaming with smiles, piloted Hezron from the front of his shop to a palatial hall covered from wall to wall with the best Damascusian carpets. There they sat down in the midst of the finest wine and palatable dishes. The maidens with apple eyes waited on them as they dined and wined in volleys of laughter and freedom.

Moza opened his mouth and said, "Hezron, do know that in another two years it would be ten years since I left my father, and it will be due for me to prove to him that I am a man who could multiply and stock gold?"

"Oh! Yes, I quite remember your father Arza said so eight years ago. Can you now prove to your father that you are a man enough?"

"Without being told," said Moza, "I left Damascus with just a bag of gold, but eight years later, I have accumulated ten."

And Hezron added, "I will feel glad also to stand before the presence of Arza and confirm to him how I have became the wealthiest men in Sidon through the practicing of his wisdom."

The two gentlemen later agreed within themselves that in two years both would travel to Damascus to pay a visit to Arza. The next day, Moza warmly waved off Hezron with his cargo of merchandise.

Chapter Three

If You Fail to Plan,
You Have Planned to Fail

Hezron reclined on his princely swing chair with the usual several—both males and females—at his attendance. He wondered for a while when he would marry and raise a family. He thought to himself, *Wealth is useless unless transferable to an heir. What use would all this gold be to me if one of my slaves inherited them?* Then he reminded himself that he was once a slave. To this he smiled gently, but none of the slaves at his attendance could guess his mind.

Then as if a spirit of freedom had ceased him, he shouted at his slaves, "You fools, must you be slaves forever?"

Shocked and surprised, the slaves gazed at him, but none had the speech to respond.

Once more, he shouted, "Do you think I have always been a rich man since my birth?"

The slaves, still in the mode of surprise, wondered where their master was going.

Then one whispered to the other, "Was our master once a slave?"

A sound of a chariot in the courtyard overshadowed the atmosphere, and one of his slaves announced the presence of the king's official, Ichabod, to Hezron. Hezron at once recovered from a philosophical fit and ushered the noble to an inner chamber, where only two of them could possibly discuss the king's business.

Though Hezron could sense the economic manner, the official accorded his warm reception, yet he proceeded to ask, "Sir, what does the king require of me?"

The official waved his hand. "I am not on the king's mission, but I have come to you for assistance as I have fallen out of favor with the king and been cast out of his presence as it is today."

Hezron remained silent for a while and asked, "If the king has no more use of you, why do you come to me?"

The visitor responded, "Sir, you could remember how I helped you in each occasion you requested some royal favor. I thought it was your turn to soothe my wounds."

Hezron retorted in a loud voice, "But I paid you for all the services you rendered to me?"

In reply, Ichabod murmured, "Sir, it's not so. I have left the king's service after twenty-five years without any gold to fall back on, but I trusted you might loan me some gold to begin the business of a merchant."

Once again, Hezron shouted back, "Nonsense! You were in the royal service for twenty-five years without anything to show for it in the form of gold, land, investments, savings, and so forth. You had better sold yourself into slavery."

The noble was too beaten to utter a word. In desperation to save a last expectation, Ichabod said, "Sir, I was young when I joined the royal service, and I never thought tomorrow would ever turn sour. I enjoyed the entire king's generosity of gold and other gifts, just as my other colleagues did. Because of our youthful age, we lavished our gold on the pretty maidens, wine, fine garments, latest-designed ornaments, chariots, and so forth, just as you would yourself. After all, what else could we have done in the midst of such affluence and young age?

People do have needs; hence, people with means like you must give generously to an old acquaintance."

However, Ichabod's story and request did not impress Hezron. To him, this was the tale often told by all those who ate their tomorrow today. They gratified all their desires as if there were no tomorrow. Such pay others without first paying themselves. Then at last there came tomorrow. They had nothing to show for their years of labor and toiling. Was this not what happened to fools? They satisfied others without considering the future. Fools were always poor people.

Hezron said to him, "There are more fools in the world than the sand of the sea. You had all the opportunities to pile up gold for yourself like a mountain, but you blew it up. Many nobles have made themselves slaves because they never cared to master their desires in the midst of plenty. While the plenty lasted, they never thought it would end one day. Alas, what you have feared most has come upon you like a thief. They have the garments, all ornaments of the latest designs, and everything that can be enjoyed. Their acquaintances loved them because they have much to benefit from them, but let the flow of their income be stopped, they are left alone to suffer. Today they enjoy, but tomorrow they are buried in the tombs of paupers.

"My good friend, I will not give you gold because you would spend it like any rich man who has investments that make gold flow to him, yet he understands the limit of how he spent. But people like you spend until all their stock of gold is exhausted." Hezron did not stop yet. "First, I will lecture you on the laws of gold. Then I would test you for five years to see if you have learned any lesson from your twenty-five years of misadventure and lack of wisdom.

"I was never born rich, but I was born the son of a slave and became one. As a slave, my father served his master Arza, the richest man in Damascus, and died a slave. Even when my father served as a slave, I was also enlisted into the army of slaves who fetched water with goatskins for the benefit of

Arza. But come to think of it, I enjoyed being a slave because my mind-set was developed and built with a slave mentality from birth.

"I saw and heard Arza teach wisdom on how to earn and stock up gold, but since I had the mentality of a slave, I never graduated this further. I remember all Arza's wisdom but didn't think they applied to a slave like me. I was only liberated from slavery and slave mentality when I saw my master's son Moza drift into slavery.

"At once, I began to recite the laws of gold as Arza taught in his school of wisdom in Damascus. They were tucked and hidden in my heart, concealed in my slave mentality. Once I began to recite them day and night, the slave mentality began to flee from my ego, and I began to want to practice them. This was how I found my freedom. If you want freedom, it will come to you, but if you don't know what you want, you will become nothing. Because I thought like a free man, freedom gave me an opportunity to be free.

The Laws of Gold

"Gold hates those who spend him on what does not earn gold. If you spend your gold on what will not generate more gold, then gold will depart from you. Thus, if you spend your gold on clothes, fashion, latest-designed objects, or ornaments such as chariots and so forth, he will depart.

"Remember: gold only wants to earn more gold for you. You can see why all the gold and gifts you received from the king in your twenty-five years of service disappeared. This fate has befallen many a wage earner. They spend all their gold in what does not earn them gold but rather momentary pleasure. They spend their money on pleasures that last them two or three years, and then they suffer the rest of their lives. They work very hard but do know how to make gold work for them. Gold only flows to those who control, prune, or curb their desires. Gold loves disciplined people who spend it in a planned manner.

"Ichabod, I wish to ask you a question. All the while you were in the king's service for twenty-five years, did you ever determine your expenditures beforehand and balance it with your income?"

The noble answered, "My colleagues and I never considered it necessary or important to determine our expenditures beforehand. Just as our income came, we spent until we sometimes went into debt."

Hezron retorted, "That is it. If you fail to plan, you have planned to fail. If you planned your expenditures beforehand, only then would you have not spent above your income. This process helps you to eliminate all expenditures that make your overshoot your income. You did not do this for twenty-five years; hence, you often went into debts. Gold increases with those who boldly control their desires. If you desired to own everything possible, you would end up owning none because when all your stock of gold would have been exhausted one day, you would live a life of a pauper."

But the noble rudely cut in, "Sir, that was exactly what happened to all my colleagues and me. Every day, we went from bazaar to bazaar, looking for the latest raiment and precious ornaments imported from faraway cities to buy. The merchants were often very generous to us by allowing us to buy on credit, knowing full well that as the king's men, we would always pay our debts. Initially, we thought the merchants were kind to us, and we often bought above our income, only to demand more gifts from those who came to seek favor from the king."

Then he stopped speaking, and Hezron took over the discussion, "The merchants did not do you any favor. All they wanted was to sell their wares, and knowing that you would not default for your status, they did their best to always make sure you bought on credit. They won't do that to just anyone.

But now that you are out of work and do not earn any copper, the merchants will no longer give you any credit. Now that you have no other income, could you as usual visit the bazaars to seek the newest things that satisfied your desires?"

"Oh no!" replied the noble.

Hezron said, "You can see that it was because you had gold then that you thought that your desires were necessaries and indispensable?"

The noble answered, "Yes."

Hezron rushed in to say, "When a fool has gold in his possession, he often thinks every desire of his is a necessity and acquires them, only to end up exhausting all his gold and becoming a poor man. When the gold was not available, they never thought anything was a necessity. But let gold come their way, and all of a sudden, their desire comes from their hiding places to consume it. You can see that desires are never real but are created by our imagination and emotions once there is gold. If you had killed your desires, you would have saved much gold while in the king's service for twenty-five years. But now you have nothing to show for the years of toiling. Do you agree with me that since you don't have any means of income at the moment, you do not also feel pressured to pursue any desires?"

Then the noble, shaking his head in regret, answered, "Hezron, you are absolutely correct. I have in fact begun to dispose of all things I accumulated over the past twenty-five years that I thought were indispensable. They mean nothing to me any longer now that I have no job. All I just want now is to survive. But to my disappointment, much of the raiment, ornaments, and so forth have no value. No one wants to buy them. When I went to the merchants, they suggested I present them as gifts to some orphanage or old people's home. When I asked why, they said they were worthless; we put much value on them when we went mad after them, but alas, we deceived ourselves."

Hezron burst out in a wild laughter, which attracted the attention of all his slaves. "That is it. The poor and working class often buy liabilities, thinking they have bought assets. They buy worthless things that have no resale value." Hezron tapped the noble gently on the shoulder. "Did you ever sit down to compute or calculate the worth of your earnings from the king those twenty-five years you spent in his service?"

The noble said he had never thought about that. "It could have been worth five bags of gold."

Hezron said, "If you had saved half of that much and invested them, you would have been one of the richest men in Sidon. But now as a poor man, you seek gold to borrow to become a merchant. It does not work like that. If you could not set apart a portion of your earnings, which amounted to five bags of gold in twenty-five years, for investment, no one would consider you wise enough to be given a loan. Everywhere you go, you would be called a fool by even those who are not wiser."

The inability of the noble to properly manage an equivalent of five bags of gold over the twenty-five year period he was in the king's service did not impress Hezron. Hezron was a very generous man and always very kind to help deserving people get started in life, but to him, Ichabod's case was useless and inexcusable.

He thought to himself, *If I gave gold to him to begin a business as a merchant, I'm dead sure that in no time, the noble would either squander the gold in his usual extravagant way of life or mismanage it, being inexperienced in the arts of the merchants.*

He looked directly at the noble's face. "I can do something to help you beyond money. It's always my desire to make all my acquaintances wealthy either by giving them wise counsel or material contribution, and you are not an exception. Before I make my proposals to you, I wish to counsel you that wealth built up gradually lives longer than wealth made in haste.

"All my life, I have never seen any who was hasty to be rich that ever got much gold. It's the wish of many that they come to sudden wealth, but if you investigate, you will see that such riches never lingered on but quickly dissipated. It's one thing to get gold, but it's another to keep it and make it work and earn for you."

By now the noble was feeling uneasy, not knowing where Hezron was heading.

Then Hezron continued, "I wish to employ you as one of my caravan drivers on a very good income and observe you for a period of five years. At the end of the time, if you have mastered the art of the merchants, I will discharge you with some handsome sum of gold to enable you to start your own business."

The noble protested, "Hezron, five years is too long. Remember that I have over twenty-five years of experience at the king's service."

Hezron said, "I don't doubt the value of your experience, but there is an experience you have never mastered, the wisdom of how to stock up gold and make it work for you. The problem with people is that they do not know how to work to make money. In fact, apart from the disabled and mentally retarded, almost everyone can labor with his hands or mind to earn a living. However, the issue is how they could keep a portion to themselves over the years and then engage it to work and earn for them. This is the experience you don't have."

The noble did agree to the truth in what Hezron said, but he answered thus, "Sir, I do agree with all you say, but I desire urgently to start something big enough to chatter for all my interest; therefore, learning a new trade at my age and with such an experience would amount to a waste."

Hezron now concluded, "Consider my counsel and offer. If acceptable to you, say a word so we could begin something."

The noble left Hezron's presence very disappointed because he thought Hezron would simply had given him some bags of gold to enable him to continue his old life of extravagance. Hezron knew that old habits were difficult to break; hence, he recommended a five-year period of training and reorientation to wane the noble of all excesses, but he was in hurry to make gold so he rejected the offer.

From Hezron's experience, no one could make lasting wealth in a hurry, but he must first begin by learning the wisdom and laws of gold. To him, anyone who got gold but did not know the laws of gold would soon lose all and become poor. However, if one knew the laws of gold, he would always make gold and let it work for him.

Hezron was never surprised at the reaction of the noble because many did not want to subject themselves to any form of discipline when they spent their gold, but they only wanted gold to squander on bloated desires. Not only that—he also knew that many in high places would be unwilling to learn new skills that would enhance their abilities to earn gold or even make them rich, so when trouble came knocking, they would tumble down the ladder. It was most difficult to change the poverty mentality cultivated over the years, so the poor got poorer and the rich got richer.

The noble thought over what Hezron said for a couple days. Then rejecting his counsel, he decided to join a gang of robbers who would waylay caravans in the wilderness. They often set up their own caravans, pretending to travel to distant lands in quest of trade, but they indeed were robbers. They prospered in their evil deeds for a while, and the maidens of the city flocked to them in the city inns and mansions richly decorated with precious ornaments.

They were passed off for genuine and successful merchants, so all in Sidon respected them. On one occasion, the gang, led by the noble, traveled into faraway lands, hurrying to haul much gold from their victims. As usual, success came their way early, but they were determined to make more faraway down the valley, where they could see a caravan put up tents to rest as night came.

The gang thought to come upon the caravan at midnight while the weary travelers were fast asleep from the journey's exhaustion. The gang delayed a little to let the darkness give them a cover. As the gang approached, the weary travelers heard the sound of hoofs at a distance. Then abandoning their pot of tea and cake of figs, they slipped into the darkness.

The gang descended on the supper and, in jubilation, helped themselves to the pot of tea and cakes. Right where they sat feasting, a frenzy of dizziness over took them, and they fell into a deep slumber.

The travelers, waiting and observing a little distance away, came later to find the gang fast asleep. Then binding their legs and hands, they took them to Damascus and sold them as slaves. Thus, the king's noble who refused to learn the wisdom and patience in earning and stockpiling gold was sold as a slave into a distant land.

Chapter Four

If You Accumulate Much Gold, Opportunities Will Come Knocking for You to Make More Gold

On many occasions, Hezron tried to convince his slaves that they could be free men, yet none could understand, but they were complacent with the comfort of his mansion. It pained him that they could not understand, but he also remembered that it took a miracle for his own slave mentality to be positively turned into that of a free man.

Every day, gold flowed into the coffers of Hezron because his investments were vast. He lacked nothing to the extent that his desire never outgrew his inflow of gold. So even the rich were careful not to run into difficulties; hence, their gold continued to grow.

Hezron seized and made good use of every opportunity that came his way. He despised nothing that could make his gold grow the more. All over the city, there were gossips that the king desired much gold to exploit the great forest of its tall trees and take them to faraway countries in exchange for more gold.

The king searched all Sidon but could find none, but Hezron had gold, much enough for such a venture. The tree fellers, dressers, and floaters of logs to distant lands must be paid in gold before the foreign purchaser would pay for the logs in gold.

The king summoned Hezron to his palace with the aides of palace officials as usual. However, what was peculiar in this case was that the king's official golden chariot was dispatched to bring Hezron to the palace.

The king personally welcomed Hezron in a warm embrace and ushered him into a palatial courtyard and then into an inner chamber decorated in gold and precious ornaments from faraway lands. This was where they sat to discuss the day's business.

The king called Hezron by name, "Hezron, you are welcome to the palace."

Hezron said with a warm smile, "May the king live forever, and may he have rule over all his subjects."

The king replied, "Thank you, Hezron." He handed over a scroll to him. "Take a look at the numerous building plans in this scroll. They are some of the magnificent buildings the richest man on earth, King Solomon of Jerusalem, wishes to put up in his realm. He has all the gold and human resources to foot the bills. Our responsibility would just be to make our timber available to him. Then in return he would pay us in gold. This business would definitely earn all you ever dreamed of. My dear Hezron, do seize this golden opportunity and multiply your stock of gold several times over. Please tell me your opinion about this affair."

Hezron opened his mouth and said humbly, "May the king live forever, and may he have rule over all his subjects. I can understand this has its roots in some foreign land. I humbly promise there is enough gold to satisfy the king's desire. One thing I must demand of the king this day is a portion of land worth three times the value of the gold as a surety if I must engage my gold in this affair. Oh, King, I know nothing about King Solomon of Jerusalem's worth and credibility, but you do know. However, fear looms over me that my gold could be lost or unduly delayed due to default. Then I will be helpless. Should this perchance happen, the portion of land would belong to me. Oh, King, I also do wish you could guarantee that in three years, by which time the venture is brought to a close, you would return to me three times the stock of gold I have put in. Oh, King, this is my humble position."

In surprise, the king stirred at Hezron for a while in admiration as if a thunderbolt struck him. He finally said, "Hezron, you speak with so much wisdom. In all my life, I never saw one such shrewd rich man who so safely guided and desired his gold grow as much. Tell me, Hezron, your background and how you came about such wisdom."

Hezron answered, "May the king live forever. I was born a slave but given the opportunely to serve a very wise master named Arza, the richest man in Damascus. I learned wisdom from him, and over the years, I diligently sought wisdom to increase my stock of gold."

The king was very happy and pleased with Hezron's acumen. He therefore did not only go into the venture on Hezron's terms but also decided to make him his chief adviser for the whole project.

In time, King Solomon of Jerusalem asked for a visit from the king of Sidon to see his projects, wealth, and majesty in order to instill confidence in all those whom he engaged in business. And the king of Sidon took Hezron along to also allay all apprehension over loss of capital and guaranteed earning. The entire realm over which King Solomon had ruled displaced the magnitude of his enormous wealth. But nowhere else was the display of extravagance of wealth and majesty most conspicuous than in Jerusalem.

Back in Sidon, copper and silver were respected mediums of exchange, but down in Jerusalem, those were often found in the streets. The king of Jerusalem treated them to a lavish welcome. They were happy and satisfied they came to Jerusalem to see with their own eyes and confirm the tales they heard back home about the grandeur of King Solomon. They watched and listened as King Solomon spoke wisdom to numerous kings and nobles who came from near and faraway lands.

With the kind permission of the king of Sidon, Hezron had the opportunity to ask King Solomon to speak some of his wisdom. Solomon spoke of how the God of his father, King David, endowed him with so much wisdom that he was a success in everything he did.

He spoke about his military might, which was responsible for the security, peace, and stability of his empire, a prerequisite for the prosperity of trade and commerce. However, what caught the immediate attention of Hezron was King Solomon's extensive and well-coordinated involvement in foreign trade. The secret of King Solomon's wealth was because he made Jerusalem a world center of commerce and trade so various kinds of goods, ornaments, jewelry, and so forth were brought in and exchanged for gold.

King Solomon also made them witness his procession to a sacrifice for Jehovah, the God of his father, King David. The temple of sacrifice was totally built of gold, as the king of Sidon and Hezron could observe. Never had they seen any God worshipped in such a lavish and extravagant manner. The visitors thought to themselves, *Maybe this is the source of his wealth, riches, power, and majesty.*

Before they left for their homeland, King Solomon presented them with so many gifts of various precious ornaments and gold. They went to their homeland with the conclusion that King Solomon was the richest man in the world.

Chapter Five

The Richest Man in Jerusalem

The time had come for Moza and Hezron to visit and pay homage to Arza, the richest man in Damascus, their mentor, father, and ex-master. When the king of Nineveh and king of Sidon learned that the richest men in their respective cities would embark on a journey to Damascus, they both wrote letters to introduce Moza and Hezron to King Sagon. Such documents would provide elaborate security to protect these men to and from Damascus, enabling them to travel in safety.

King Sagon of Damascus, on his own part, evolved elaborate measures to welcome these rich men into his city. For Moza, it was time to prove to his father Arza that he could earn and stock up gold with the wisdom he inscribed in the five scrolls for him. Then on the part of Hezron, it would be a memorable reunion with his ex-slave master whose wisdom transformed the mentality of a slave to lift him up to become the richest man in Sidon. Each of the men, Moza and Hezron, rode on their own golden chariots accompanied by a caravan a mile long.

The soldier and guides who were at their rear and front stretched a distance of five miles apart. The caravans marched on day after day, but at intervals, they set up camps and rested. At once, they could see the huge winding wall of Damascus enclosing the city. Then as they descended into some valleys and then plains, the city became out of their view.

The journey continued until they approached within a mile of the gates of Damascus, where slaves and free men lined the king's highway to welcome the richest men in Sidon and Nineveh and not the ex-slave and ex-extravagant son.

The past was no longer the question; therefore, everybody jubilated about what Moza and Hezron were now. People often lived in the now and not the past. These were the acclaimed richest men of the world, and that was enough knowledge to excite the crowd to sing, wave, and dance. And Moza and Hezron lavished so much gifts on the crowd that some had enough to pay debts, build up new venture, and even buy their freedom. They rode straight to the palace of Arza, the richest man in Damascus and father of Moza.

Arza hugged his son warmly and did the same to Hezron, the ex-slave. How times had changed things. Arza was now an old man fully greyed at the head. Several slaves and maidens milled around to offer them the best services of wine and the finest meals in Damascus.

Hezron could recognize some of the slaves. They were his colleagues when he was a slave, but he was now free and rich while these were still wasting away their future as slaves. He smiled warmly at them, but as a tradition, they were only to be seen and not heard.

Arza looked straight at Hezron's face. "Now that you have become the richest man in Sidon, maybe you have learned some new wisdom that could help us increase our stocks of gold once more."

Hezron reclined on his golden seat, "Yes, Mr. Arza," calling him by name, which he never dared do while he was his slave. But now, time and fortunes had changed the status of Hezron. "I indeed have a lot of wisdom to share with you and Moza. I learned wisdom from you, and I became rich in gold.

While a slave with you, I listened and learned as you taught the free men the laws of gold.

"I also did learn as a slave to your son Moza as his stock of gold dwindled without due diligence. Then he sold me to a new master. I departed in tears because your son Moza did lavish his stock of gold and turned a poor man. There and then my mind was awoken, and I remembered the wisdom you taught and inscribed in the five scrolls. And I began to recite each from then on. These delivered me from slave mentality to become a rich free man. As my stock of gold grew, I guided my capital against loss and gambles, and I became rich and secured.

"My gold became so much as I seized every good opportunity that came my way, and I got ever richer when more opportunities did come and I learned new wisdom. Through the king of Sidon, I learned I could also earn much gold from foreign trade. The king brought ventures from faraway lands, but I was careful to ask his guarantees, which were three times my capital. In this I profited much. My visit to a foreign king named Solomon in the city of Jerusalem in the company of the king of Sidon also did reinforce my confidence in foreign trade as much source of gold.

"King Solomon demonstrated to the king of Sidon and I much wisdom, and we were indeed convinced that the manner he sacrificed to the deity he called Jehovah, the God of his father, King David, is the source of his great wealth, just like he explained to us. I do here confirm that King Solomon is indeed the richest man I have ever seen in the entire world. I have since begun to sacrifice only to this God called Jehovah, whose golden temple is located at a majestic city called Jerusalem. King Solomon did confirm that anyone from any nation who did come to pray in the temple of Jehovah gets his requests met."

Then Arza cut in rudely, "Hezron, do you indeed believe that the gods do influence riches and do it generously to those who extravagantly sacrifice to them? If you are positive, why has the Damascus god not dealt thus with me?"

Hezron replied, "Even in Sidon, we have gods, but none is reputed to be a sure and guaranteed source of wealth. But the god whose temple is located at Jerusalem does, according to tales, endow much wealth to the Jews and all who sacrifice to him. The testimony of Solomon and all that the king of Sidon and I saw in Jerusalem pointed to this."

Arza, taking a very deep breath while smiling, said, "Well, I have heard rumors about this strange and incredible God and King Solomon. I would in no time prove the veracity of these claims about Jehovah by visiting the city of Jerusalem." Turning to Moza, Arza announced, "Tonight, King Sagon of Damascus has summoned all his nobles, slaves, and free men to the great court in his palace to listen to the man who has become the richest man in Nineveh. With the king's kind permission, Moza would give a speech to motivate the people. However, before we proceed to the king's palace, since your departure, I have indeed also learned new wisdom. Wealthy is vanity and useless if not passed on to one's descendants. There is no doubt that one's descendants may not have learned the wisdom of earning wealth and stocking it up. In this wise, I, by research and wisdom, have discovered how this can be practiced. Listen to these.

1. As early as possible, engage children in all technicalities of your business.
2. Teach your children from youth directly about your business. This must be his or her education.
3. Let the children learn a Spartan and disciplined way of life. Luxury will spoil them early.
4. While they are young, put them as observers in committees that make decisions in the organization.
5. Make them take some responsibilities early and graduate them to additional obligations over time.

6. As they grow up in the business, teach them to make decisions and develop confidence in them.

At the end of their discussion, Arza led the way to the king's palace, where a huge crowd was waiting to hear wisdom from Moza, the richest man in Nineveh.

Chapter Six

Riches Brings Fame and Recognition from the Public and Even Kings

The great courtyard of the king was crowded, and there was not enough room to sit. So more people stood than sat in readiness to hear the wisdom Arza taught to his son Moza to make him the richest man in Nineveh.

The king of Damascus had solicited the wisdom of Arza to teach wisdom to a select few to make them rich, but never had there been such a testimony of enormous wealth being learned from the application of that wisdom as with Moza. The king of Damascus therefore requested a lecture from Moza that the whole populace of this city might embrace the practicability and truth of Arza's wisdom. Quite simply, the king of Damascus wanted all citizens in his realm rich so that, by aggregation, Damascus might be even richer. The king reasoned that if all the people were rich, so would the city be more prosperous.

Moza led the procession of nobles toward the rostrum. The people greeted and shouted in wild applause. Then one of the king's officials handed a bullhorn to Moza.

Moza shouted at the top of his voice, "May the king live forever and make Damascus the richest city in the world!"

The crowd rose to their feet, waving and cheering, drowning the voice of Moza. He waited for their voices to calm. Then he began in a warm and gentle voice to narrate how, by applying the wisdom of Arza, his father and the richest men in Damascus, he became the richest man in Nineveh.

"Any slave or free man can learn the wisdom of Arza and become rich in gold. The wisdom my father taught is simple to apply, yet fools will despise it for its simplicity. I was a fool until I learned and practicalized the wisdom. My father gave me a bag of gold and five scrolls of wisdom. Between gold and wisdom, the majority will choose gold. I chose gold, and because I despised wisdom, I squandered all my gold. And the day my gold bag became empty, I was compelled to resort to wisdom. I thought to myself, *All fools resort to wisdom only when they have squandered their gold.*"

The crowd bust out in wild laughter.

Moza continued, "When all my gold expired, I became a poor man. I did not easily embrace poverty, having lived in luxury as the son of the richest man in Damascus, yet I had no choice but to lead such a life. All my friends ran away from me, first the maidens and followed by all other acquaintances.

"At the peak of poverty, even my slaves despised me, and so in misery, I sold them to live a life tucked far away from the public view. In my state, I came to understand that even a slave is guaranteed a minimal life as the master benefits from his labor, but the poor has no one to care for him, for he must fend for himself. I also found that riches could buy friends, love, favor, and so forth. But the poor have nothing to recommend him. The rich man is happy, bold, and heard by all, but the poor in hunger even begs from a slave.

"I experienced the shame of poverty, lack, hunger, and inferiority complex. Then I remembered the pleasurable and confident life I had enjoyed when I had gold, so I decided to turn back to wisdom so I could regain my freedom. By now, I hated poverty and its consequences. Each morning I woke up, I cursed poverty."

Once more, the crowd went wild in applause. They rose up, raised their hands, and cursed poverty. Moza waved his hand to calm them, but the crowd was defiant. Finally they calmed.

Moza then went further, "If I had not tasted affluence, I would not have known the difference between it and poverty, and because of that, I was most determined to become rich once more. And determination is the right word. Mark this statement. Only absolute determination can deliver from poverty. In my desperation to become rich, I turned to the five scrolls of Arza. I wish to explain these in simple and plain language to you so you might not have any excuse to remain poor and thereby accumulate much gold.

1. You may be born a slave or poor, yet you can accumulate much gold by wisdom.
2. Be determined not to remain poor, and be determined to become rich.
3. Work hard and be diligent in all you engage in; by so doing, you can become an expert.
4. If you work hard and diligently for a master, you will learn to work hard.
5. Save a portion your earnings as the income comes. Be disciplined enough to do this for years. You may save 10, 15, or 20 percent or even more depending on your efforts.
6. Prune or restrict your desires and expenditures. Then you will continue to save more gold.
7. Learn that expenditures are mere habits built on emotions that will eventually lead to poverty.
8. Invest your savings to earn you income. Never stop at that. Invest earnings of your income until your

savings and earnings begin to earn more gold for you. In other words, let your gold work for you. This is the secret of the rich. The poor work with their physical strength to earn gold, but the rich earn by allowing their gold to work for them.

9. Never gamble with your savings or try to earn quick money, or else you will be defrauded of your savings.

10. Run away from promises of high earnings, for many have lost all their capital in such a manner.

11. Never invest your gold without the help of an expert, except if you are an expert yourself.

12. Remember that your capital is your life because you have built it up all your life. So never gamble with it; else you will lose it.

13. As your gold grows, learn to recognize opportunities so your gold could earn you more gold.

14. Learn that the poor wishes to satisfy all desires, but even the rich do not satisfy all their desires.

15. The more gold you have, the more gold will flow to you.

16. Gold flows to those who don't gamble with it but are concerned to invest it wisely.

"I learned this wisdom from my father, Arza, the richest man of Damascus. When I became a poor man, I turned to learn and zealously apply this wisdom. At first, they looked difficult to practice, but when I turned and surveyed the ignominious consequences of poverty, I was more determined than ever to apply the wisdom of Arza to my affairs daily.

"Then the days, months, and years rolled by. I began to reap much gold. My gold began to work for me. I was also trialed when I reinvested the earnings from my gold, which also began to earn me more gold. As much as possible, I reinvested my earnings, so I earned much gold since I had much gold working for me.

"I had my failures, but I only called them setbacks. Each time I failed, I turned again to the wisdom of Arza and became more equipped to move into the future. You see, Arza only called failures as setbacks. He considered those who quit their quest to earn much gold as real failures. I kept this truth glued to my heart, and when I failed, I never quit but saved again to invest or put my gold into wiser earning ventures.

"Gold wants you to seek him right now so he can also, by reciprocity, flow to you. Every delay to put aside a tenth or more of your income is evidence of the absence of rigid determination to accumulate gold. Gold is eager to work and earn for anyone who would put portion of his earning aside and then invest it. I became the richest man in Nineveh because I put the wisdom that made Arza, my father, the richest man in Damascus, into immediate practice. I would also wish to mention to you the richest man in Sidon. He is here with me and would say one or two words to you."

As Moza beckoned for Hezron to mount the rostrum, the crowd never stopped to clap and jubilate.

Hezron greeted the crowd, and the response was spontaneous. He cleared his throat and began to speak, "I am a living testimony of the wisdom of Arza. As the richest man in Sidon, I can confidently recommend the wisdom of Arza as the last hope of the slave and free man. I was born a slave and served several masters—Arza, Moza, and so forth—yet today I am the richest man in Sidon. When I began to learn the wisdom of Arza, I recited them to myself in the morning, noon, and night. There I found that gold is always willing to search out all those who desire him.

"In no time, I became a free man because I desired so, to accumulate much gold. What you desire will come to you, no matter how many years may pass by. If you desire to accumulate much gold like the richest man in Damascus, so you would be. As one born a slave at the services of several masters, my desire for freedom and accumulating gold was strong. And one day after several years, I became what I was determined to be. You too can also become free and the owner of much gold if you apply the wisdom of Arza."

Chapter Seven

Only a Fool Will Fail and Quit

"When I, Ichabod, heard that the richest man in Sidon would visit Damascus in the company of the richest man in Nineveh, I knew it was my last opportunity to become a free man. I had known Hezron as the king's official in Sidon. There, I did him a lot of favor, and he was kind to as many when I was in the king's service.

"When I fell out of favor with the king, Hezron was one old friend I consulted for counsel, but I did not heed his wisdom. I followed after the ruffians and the get-rich-quick crowd. It worked for a while, and I tasted the great life of the affluent, but the long arm of the law later caught up with me, and I was sold into slavery in Damascus.

"That day, as the procession of chariots passed by to herald the arrival of Hezron and Moza, I watched closely to catch the glance of Hezron. My ambition was hot in my heart. As he passed by, I would call him by name at the top of my voice to buy me my freedom. It was a last opportunity, so I was desperate enough to attract his attention to me even in the midst of such a crowd.

"I knew I must not miss this golden opportunity to catch up with Hezron; else he would be lost into the official protocol of the king. And no one—not to mention a slave—could be allowed to see him. Moza was leading the procession. *No doubt*, I said to myself, *this is not the Hezron I knew.*

"More ordinary chariots came by. Then all of a sudden, another golden chariot was coming along, and no one need tell me that Hezron was in this one. I could very well recognize him from a distance. As he got right in front of me, I made a desperate dash at this golden chariot.

"It came to a scratching halt to avoid crushing me to death. Then the solders swarmed all over me and pulled me off, but I continued to shout 'Hezron! Hezron! Hezron!' He heard his name and ordered the solders to let go of me so he might have a better view of who I was.

"He cautiously approached, and looking straight at my face, he recognized me and screamed my name, 'Ichabod! Were you not the king's noble back at Sidon?' I answered back. 'Yes, sir, I was.' But before he could say anything further, I continued hastily, 'Please, sir, I have been sold into slavery. Have mercy on me, an old friend, and buy me my freedom.'

"He immediately ordered me to climb into the backseat of his chariot. Then the procession continued toward the mansion of Arza. Once in Arza's palace, he ordered new garments be given me and weighed a few pieces of gold as the price of my freedom. Holding the purchase receipt at my face, he tore it into shreds and cast it into the fireplace. Then he whispered at me, 'Today you have become a free man.' My heart beat faster and faster while tears began to roll down my face. Then I said, 'Hezron, thanks for a favor to an old friend. Be good to them because you never know who will be of help to you in some distant future.'

"He handed me over to his officials as he went in to dine and wine with Moza and Arza. Then the smartly dressed slaves moved in a single file to serve Arza, Moza, Hezron, and other nobles. Instinctively, I joined them. We had made the third round of service when Hezron looked and found me amongst the slaves.

"I smiled at him, but he stared at me and shouted to the hearing of all the others, 'You fool, you are now a free man. Why yet perform the routine of slaves anymore? Ichabod, you must forever cast off the slave mentality from you; else you once more sell yourself into slavery.' I stood miserably gazing at him and asked, 'How can I do this?' Hezron said, 'You sit there and let the slaves serve you for once.'

"I obeyed and sat with the nobles. Then the slaves began to serve me. Then I remembered that I was once a noble in the king's palace in Sidon. Later, Hezron called me aside and handed some scrolls and a quarter bag of gold. He said, 'Here is wisdom and gold. You must learn wisdom before gold can continuously flow to you. Never you begin with gold, but always start with wisdom. Wisdom will never fail you, but gold can if you lack wisdom.'

"Then I asked, 'What can I do that I will not fail, seeing that this is my last opportunity?' He said, 'Take note of these pieces of wisdom, and you will not fail.'

1. Work very hard and at long hours in whatever you are engaged in. Make hard work your friend. You will discover a secret as you do this.
2. Learn skills, not just one, two, or even more. You may have occasion to fall back on them to earn wages or as a point of judgment.
3. Have a desire to accumulate gold.
4. Never involve in illegal deals that could send you to prison.
5. Save a tenth or more of your earnings because this is all that you can show for your labor. You will be proud and happy at this.
6. Control your desires and reduce your expenditures or anything that does not earn you income. Make this a point of duty, and you will earn and save more gold.

7. This gold piece I have given you is your capital. Never put it at risk by gambling, or involving yourself in get-rich-quick schemes, or engaging in ventures you have no knowledge of. Risky ventures will rob you of your capital, which you may not easily get back. Consider the act of providence that cumulated in you receiving these pieces of gold. How many are chanced to receive such in life? Some never do in their lifetimes. The capital is therefore your life. In loaning it out, make sure you do so to only those who could repay without fail and delay. By investment, do those only that have no risk of it being lost. Therefore, shun risky ventures even with promises of handsome returns.

8. Never blame your income for your predicament. Be determined to save a tenth or more monthly. You could always set aside greater portions with more determination. When you do this at small income, you will also be enabled to do such when your income is increased. Avoid the pitfall of many whose desires increase with growing income. Such would desire more income, yet their desires grew to consume all.

9. Even the king could not satisfy all his desires, and so is Arza, the richest man in Damascus. The lesson here is to never let your desires consume all your income; else you will have nothing to show for all your life labor. Learn here again that the poor wants all things, but the rich do not desire all things because they know that if they did, their desires would consume all their income. Be wise not to let emotions or peer groups dictate your desires, but always strive to set aside a portion of your earnings at regular intervals such as a month and so forth.

10. If your house is in order—that is, if you had acquired skills or put away a portion of your income over the years—opportunities will come seeking you. Great

opportunities await those who are prepared and ready to grab them. An opportunity to team up to exploit a situation or buy some expensive products at rock-bottom price and so forth will one day come knocking at the door of a man prepared for it. Recognize opportunities, and act fast.

11. The poor get poorer and are entangled in its web because all they acquire make them spend more of their income. The rich always buy what assists them to make more gold. The desires of the poor drown them, but the rich suppress their desires. The poor wants to act and spend like the rich out of inferiority complex so they will be thought to be rich. No one gets rich by spending like the rich, but by saving and investing like the rich.

12. Always invest your accumulated gold with expert advice unless you have a thorough and technical knowledge of the venture. Even in such situations, seek a second view so you do not stand a chance of losing your capital. Remember that your capital is your life. It is worth the while to pay for expert advice. By so doing, you have sound advice and minimize huge losses at little cost.

13. Very often, some fellow might say that this or that business is very profitable. Don't be lured or carried away by such and invest your hard-earned gold. I can say that all ventures can be profitable if you know the secrets. Every success has secrets. Find out such secrets by a thorough investigation even with the help of an expert before any action. If you have the choice, and even in all cases, don't learn by experience. Rather, learn by the experience of others who had failed and now succeeded. You will save money and time and have a guaranteed success.

14. If you have much gold flow into your store, you can satisfy more of your desires. But much gold will only flow to you when you have invested all these days. Much gold takes much days, months, and years to build up. The sooner you begin to build up your gold, the better. If you have not started, you may never do, so begin now.

15. Invest your gold, but don't eat its earnings. Then reinvest such earnings again, and in no time, a river of gold will begin to flow to you. You make your gold work for you. Make earning its children also work for you. Also invest its grandchildren to work for you.

16. Your slaves are your most valuable possession. Motivate them, and you will get the best out of them. Be strong willed, and focus on dealing with your slaves, but allow their initiatives to be put to work for you, and much gold will flow to your stock.

"After Hezron had thus spoken, he asked an official to take a chariot with me and drive me to the city center. The official did just as he said. With the scroll of wisdom in my left hand and a quarter bag of gold in the right, I walked into a brand-new life to prove the wisdom inscribed in the scrolls. I stood still and paused for a moment with various ideas rumbling in my heart, but I took little or no notice of them because I was fighting the last battle of life."

Chapter Eight

The Captive of Desires

Our desires drive us to want to acquire various things. When we obey our desires and acquire things above our income, we run into debts and poverty. It is important to know that no one, no matter how rich, can satisfy all his desires, but strange enough, poor people always try to do so.

A very strong force drives mortal man to acquire his desires. So strong is this force that many do think twice or make budgets before they incur expenditures. A man who spends all his income on desires is a prisoner of his desires.

The fire that ignites desires is the human character to want to be like his peers at all costs. After all, it's normal or natural for us to spend, act, dress, and even excel like our peers. When you join the excessive desires of a husband to his wife's, the answer will be debts and poverty. It is good when we begin to teach our children early how to curb desires.

Anyone who wants to get rich must first learn how to curb desires and leave a balance to be saved in his income. It will surprise you to know that there is no income that is so small that it cannot be budgeted. The same is also true. There is no income too big for desire to consume.

Many people's desires often grow to cover their incomes, leaving none to be saved. Even when the income is increased,

increased desires will consume it. I want to define a poor man as one whose income is consumed by his desires. Your status now and in the future is not dependent on your income, but it's on how you can curb your desires to make savings for a rainy day or future.

It's not what you get but what you keep. If you have a very big income but consumed all in your desires, tell me something: Are you better than one who earns less than a quarter yet has good savings? Now amongst the two, who is rich, and who is poor? Can you see the light? It's not the size of your income that makes you rich or poor; it's what you keep.

The one who is a prisoner of desire cannot keep anything despite his income, and one day, if that source of income dries up, he has nothing to fall back on. Even when there is a promotion or a new job with increased income, the captive of desire will always have new desires to consume any increment.

Over 90 percent of people all over the world are captives of desires. As you read on, you might as well ask yourself if you are a prisoner of desires. If you can discover who you are, it will be easy for you to quit poverty.

Captives of Desires Have Some Common Symptoms

1. They are always broke every month no matter how much they are paid. Have you ever seen when a manager is broke every month but the messenger has savings? This is what I, the author, am saying. An extravagant higher-salary earner borrows from a more prudent worker.

2. The captive of desires will never budget his income and expenditures until he has overshot his income. When his income is finished, he then tries to figure out what happened. It's too late.

3. The captive of desire runs into debts even for his day-to-day expenditure. When his income is increased,

he runs into more debts. He spends in anticipation of income, and when the income arrives, his account is zero because he overspends.

4. The captive of desire has little or no savings, no matter his income. He will overdraw his account and always remain in the red. He lives on credit.

5. The prisoner of desire does not make a stable staff.

6. The captive of desire has nothing to fall back on when his job is no more. He cannot survive unemployment even for one month but for external help.

7. The prisoner of desires never tries to adjust but always is arguing and justifying his oversized expenditure.

Chapter Nine

Only a Change Can Bring Financial Freedom

Most people complain all their lives about an insufficiency of their finances, which goes on from year to year. The same issue they had some thirty years back is the same they have today. I have found out that more than 90 percent of people make the complaint of insufficiency of their finances all through their lives.

A close look at some people's finances shows an increase over the years, yet they still make the same complaint of financial insufficiency. There are two closely related reasons why many people do not have enough not to talk about a surplus to invest to make them rich:

1. Too many people are too rigid to change their patterns of expenditures.
2. Many people think their problem is the size of their income.

When you look at change in the pattern of expenditures, it is obviously the reason why many are not rich. People often take things for granted and therefore spend their income without a plan.

Anyone who spends without a plan is bound to be poor. Look at the life of people who have become financially independent. They have a planned pattern of expenditures every month or so. When you adhere to this pattern of planned expenditure, you can have a surplus to save and invest. If you don't plan your expenditures, you will always be broke and run into debts. God wants you to spend your money with wisdom.

I want to tell you that no one on earth can satisfy all his desires, no matter how rich that person may be; hence, rich people plan all their expenditures, but poor people don't. By poor here, I mean people who don't have savings and investments.

You may be earning a very big income right now, but if you don't have financial freedom, you can become a slave of your desire and then run into debts. That may not be the end of it, no matter how good your income is. If you don't save and invest, what will be your situation if you lose your job or eventually retire?

A man without planned expenditures will regret this in the very nearest future. Remember that it's not how much you earn now but how much you keep that matters. If you were to earn $1 million today and keep it for the future, you would have financial freedom.

If a man were to squander all the million today, a person who earned $10,000 monthly and saved $200,000 over the years, which he invested, is far better off. If you make millions today, you can become a poor man tomorrow, but a more careful fellow who earned far less but keeps much will be a rich man tomorrow.

A very great mistake people often make is for them to think the same good opportunities will present themselves repeatedly. You must take it that opportunity knocks but once and you must grab if fast; else it will run away forever. When you have the opportunity, make the best use of it.

I want you to consider that the present situation you are in now is an opportunity you must use wisely. Don't wait for tomorrow. If you do so, you are risking your future. If you can make the best use of today, you will make a better use of tomorrow. However, if you cannot master today, a greater disaster may be waiting for you tomorrow. If you plan your expenditures today, you will be a master of all your future expenses.

Let us come to the question of an increased income. Anyone who is captive of his desires will always spend his increased income on new desires. If he doubles the salary of the captive of desires, he would double his expenditure. If he triples his income, he would also triple his expenditure. A man who is broke at $10,000 will no doubt also be broke at $100,000.

You can see why increased income does not determine poverty or riches. What determines riches is your ability to plan your income and pay yourself between 10 to 30 percent of all your earnings to be invested and reinvested. You invest and reinvest what you earn from your original investment.

When you continue this, you will watch your riches grow. This is the great secret of the rich. They get their money to work for them. You must do this to get rich.

Chapter Ten

Take a Practical Step Now

One must do everything possible to lose himself from the web of entanglement of desires, the major source of poverty. A man who cannot control his desires will always be unhappy all his life. Many of the things we often call desires are nothing but habits cultivated all the years that we can easily do away with.

We can do away with very many things, and our status, health, and career may be unaffected. Begin by drawing up a budget of your income and expenditures. If you have never done it before, you must begin it now. Don't wait until tomorrow; let your prosperity begin this very moment. You can kill your desires by stepping down your expenditures by strict adherence to a budget that must leave you a surplus of 10 to 30 percent of your income.

You could reduce the cost of your meals in terms of quality or changing your source of purchase. You may choose a cheaper means of transportation and source of clothing. You can always scrutinize each expenditure in your budget and find an alternative.

Remember: if you don't change and reduce your desires and leave a surplus, you are on the way to poverty. The poor man is not respected in the society. The earlier you kill your desires, the better and easier it is for you to make a surplus, which you could now invest to earn you extra income.

I want you to take a pen and a piece of paper. Write down your income very boldly on the top right-hand corner. On the left-hand side, I want you to list all the different kinds of expenditures you engage in daily, weekly, or monthly, as the case may be. Write down all your expenses, no matter how little they may be.

List how much you spend on rice, beans, plantain, fish, beef, pepper, tomatoes, onions, vegetable oil, eggs, vegetables, medicines, sweets, books, newspapers, new clothes, shoes, soft drinks, fruits, rent, transport, gifts, education, electronics, car, furniture, holiday, and so forth.

Now, I want to tell you why you must list all your expenditures. You must look at them critically and see the ones you can outright cancel or reduce. Remember: your objective will be to save between 10 and 30 percent of your income. In all cases, you can always make cuts that will result in sizable savings.

Do not protect or defend any expenditure. You can always make a saving if you look at your expenditures with a progressive eye. You will find out some of your expenses do not necessarily contribute anything to your well-being. Know that if you can succeed in reducing your expenditures and saving between 10 and 30 percent, you are on the way to becoming a rich man.

Half of what you eat contributes nothing to good health. Half of expenditures on fashion only drain your income. A new car is good, but how long will it remain new? Three years? Then you demand another? Remember: whatever you save and invest now will yield more income in the future to make you rich.

Once more, consider the fact that if you were unemployed or without any income, your desire would be almost zero. A man without an income would not demand a new car or house or some latest designer wear.

We must not deceive ourselves. Most of the things we desire and call necessity are borne out of emotions of the pressure to meet up with what is in vogue. People just want to do what others are doing and so drive themselves into poverty.

But when there is new employment, a second job, or an increment, all of a sudden there will be courage and a new desire to visit the showrooms and purchase the latest in clothes, electronics, cars, housing, and so forth. We must therefore not allow our feelings and emotions to deceive us into squandering our income.

The majority of people, the 95 percent, follow this path and spend all they earn to show off that they are rich. But the truth is that you are not rich because you buy what all the others or the rich buy. You can only be judged rich in the true sense if your money is working to earn for you and not when you labor to earn.

In other words, to be rich you must have enough investment in shares, real estate, or some other investments earning income for you. This is different from the normal conviction that something could happen one day and you could land a huge sum of money that would propel you to the millionaire's club.

Well, this could happen, but if you don't learn to control your desires now, the likelihood is that you will follow the usual pattern when such great opportunities arise, and you will squander as you've done in the past. To be rich could be systematically done by your setting aside a portion of your income on a regular basis or wisely investing in such.

www.ingramcontent.com/pod-product-compliance
Lightning Source LLC
Chambersburg PA
CBHW030914180526
45163CB00004B/1822